the DYNAMICS *of*
WORSHIP

JAMES P. GILLS, M.D.

CREATION
HOUSE

THE DYNAMICS OF WORSHIP by James P. Gills, M.D.
Published by Creation House
A Charisma Media Company
600 Rinehart Road
Lake Mary, Florida 32746
www.charismamedia.com

Unless otherwise noted, Scripture quotations are from the New American Standard Bible. Copyright © 1960, 1962, 1968, 1971, 1972, 1973, 1975, 1977 by the Lockman Foundation. Used by permission. (www.Lockman.org)

Scripture quotations marked KJV are from the King James Version of the Bible.

Design Director: Bill Johnson
Cover design by Karen Grindley

Library of Congress Control Number: 2004112090
International Standard Book Number: 978-1-59185-657-3
E-book ISBN: 978-1-61638-725-9

17 18 19 20 21 — 11 10 9 8 7
Printed in the United States of America

To all who desire a deeper walk with the Lord.

With love.

To fall in love with God is the highest of all romances.

To seek Him is the greatest of all adventures.

To find Him is the greatest human achievement.

AUTHOR UNKNOWN

ACKNOWLEDGMENTS

Looking back, I see that I have often moved in the wrong direction. I have been a legalist, I have been an existentialist, and although I have tried to stick to the Word and ask for an anointing in it, I still have failed to fully worship God. Therefore, I would like to acknowledge those people who have been intercessors for me during the times when I have tried to learn how to worship.

I also wish to acknowledge at this time the people who have taught me how to appreciate God, to be totally satisfied in Him, and so, to receive peace. One of these people is John Piper, and another one is his predecessor, Jonathan Edwards. They spoke of the person of Jesus Christ. They distinguished between religion and the relationship with our Creator and Savior. I would like to acknowledge these two men with the deepest respect.

Most of us never appreciate our mothers enough, though we should. They bore us in pain and then raised us. We never appreciate the magnitude of God's creative act that brought everything and everyone into being. We never think about, let alone appreciate, the amazing "microchip," the zygote, which is a microscopic particle in our mama's tummy nine months before we are born. This "microchip" is a single cell, yet it contains more information than two hundred NYC telephone books. This information is powerful enough to develop and control two hundred types of tissues and integrate them into a functioning human being. Then, with complexity greater than any computer system, the information originating in the zygote controls and maintains the body. For example, it controls our pancreas as it responds to dietary intake, and it does this from before we are born until we pass into eternity.

Matthew 22:37–39 teaches us that the greatest commandment is to love God—to appreciate God—with all our hearts. Our greatest fault, then, surely must be not appreciating and worshiping Him with all our hearts. By learning to worship with passion, we can grow in fulfilling this greatest of all quests—to find our complete satisfaction in glorifying Him.

As I look at my life, I think of the greatest human disease—the fact that I worried rather than worshiped. I know that a spirit of thanksgiving removes the worry and allows me to worship God. The ultimate worship is absolute appreciation of Him. Enoch was probably one of the best worshipers, and he was translated into God's presence. I doubt that even Enoch really appreciated to one millionth of the extent he should have what God had done for him. How much farther have I fallen short of worshiping and appreciating God? Our job is truly to appreciate Him rather than worry. With my biggest illness being worry and my biggest shortcoming being lack of appreciation, it is only appropriate that I write a book on worship and say, "Let me appreciate You in worship, so that I am translated into Your presence!"

—James P. Gills, M.D.

TABLE OF CONTENTS

Part Three: All-Consuming Fire

FOREWORD

Dr. Jim Gills' book on worship is a welcome resource to this field to which the body of Christ is happily returning. I have enjoyed reading and rereading it and making it available to those I teach on praise and worship. The reader will find the presentation a delicate combination of concept and practice, technique and spirit, and knowledge and inspiration. The one who reads it is left with the sense that worship is the supreme recourse on planet Earth and when exercised, becomes a supreme resource. Having studied extensively on this subject, I find ample cause to commend this fine work to any and all believers.

—JACK TAYLOR
AUTHOR, *THE HALLELUJAH FACTOR*

PART ONE:

KINDLING

Chapter One

PRELUDE TO WORSHIP

WINTER.

Biting winds whistled through the deserted streets of a quaint, northern town. The temperature continued to drop, but that failed to deter one lone man from venturing outside. Heavily bundled to protect himself against the subzero weather, with the ends of his plaid, woolen neck scarf flapping in the wind, Jake Matthews walked with steady, brisk strides. His hunched shoulders and forward lean gave him the appearance of a man on a mission. Who else would be out on such a fearsome night?

As Jake pressed onward to a destination known only to himself, he spotted a trembling, emaciated dog cowering for shelter behind a telephone pole. Something drew him a step closer. He couldn't be sure, but it looked like a child had played a cruel prank on the poor dog.

Jake squinted. Sure enough, a tin can was tied to the dog's tail and the rope was wrapped around the pole several times. In his frantic struggles to get free from the can, he must have run back and forth from pole to tree, all to no avail. Finally, with one last desperate dash in a circle, the animal had sealed his fate. Without a break in the weather, which was unlikely, he would make his last stand entangled around the telephone pole.

What a sorry sight! Jake thought as he stared at the dog. Compassion tugged at his heart. For the moment, he forgot how cold he was. Drawing closer still, he paused and inspected the creature. *He's skinny, all right. Looks miserable. Bald patches in his coat. A stray, no doubt.*

Jake stooped down, reached out his hand, and called to the dog. Suspicious at first, and for good reason, the dog overcame his fears and gradually approached. Inch by slow inch he crept forward, whining with each step. Gently, Jake reached out his hand and stroked the frightened animal, all the while speaking kind words. After removing the string and tin can from his tail, the man lifted the dog up, opened his overcoat, and tucked the bedraggled animal inside for the journey back home.

Arriving at last, Jake went into the house and explained to his wife how he found the half-starved little dog on the street. He urged her, "Please, sweetheart, put a blanket in the corner of the kitchen by the heater, where it's warm. We'll take care of him, at least for tonight." He looked down and shook his head. "He would've died if I'd left him out in the cold."

Mary smiled to herself, knowing her husband's soft heart for strays. One night would never be enough. She returned with a suitable blanket, and together they lovingly placed the still-quivering creature upon it. He whimpered softly. They offered a delicious bowl of warm milk and bread, followed by some scraps from the evening meal. The famished dog devoured the feast. For the first time in many months, he wagged his tail (with caution) for the unusual kindness bestowed on him.

The next day, as Jake and Mary awoke to the early morning sunlight, the dog greeted his benefactors with a slightly more enthusiastic wag of his tail. As the couple exchanged a quick glance, they reached a decision. The dog, though not much to look at in his present state, had found a home.

"What should we name him, dear?" Jake asked. "He must have a name if he's to be part of the family." They were both silent for a few moments, then stared at the dog and at each other.

Mary volunteered with a chuckle, "The way he looks, 'Old Bones' might suit him fine."

"True, he's not much of a prize right now," he answered. "You just wait, though! In a month or so he'll look like he's got royal blood in him." He paused and thought a moment. "How about 'Monarch' for a name? Rather regal-sounding, don't you think? Besides, that's the name of a butterfly. You know how different *they* look from the caterpillar that spins a cocoon!"

Monarch he became.

Days and weeks passed since the new addition to the family. Time revealed an incredible metamorphosis taking place in the old dog. His eyes became clearer, his nose grew cool and moist, and his tail wagged vigorously whenever anyone even glanced his way. More remarkable, though, was his coat. The silky, russet-colored fur glistened in the sunlight that streamed in through the window onto his favorite napping spot. What a change in Monarch! After lots of good food and tender, loving care, Jake and Mary could scarcely recognize the fine-looking animal as the same miserable stray of four weeks earlier.

Each afternoon at about four-thirty, Monarch whined and scratched at the door to go outside. He trotted to the end of the walk, sat by the gate, and waited for his master to come home from work. The sound of the family car coming up the street was etched clearly in his memory. As soon as the familiar noise reached his ears, he would begin barking excitedly, thumping his tail with wild abandon.

Joy...joy! Master was home!

Then, when Monarch heard the car door slam shut, he could restrain himself no longer. He ran in circles and bounded about, almost knocking over his beloved Jake as he came through the gate. From that moment on, master and dog remained inseparable for the rest of the evening.

One night after dinner, Jake was snoozing in his favorite easy chair with his arm dangling over the armrest. Monarch lay nearby in utter bliss. Suddenly, Jake awakened to something wet nuzzling his hand. As he leaned over the side of the chair, his gaze met two of the most loving eyes any dog ever had for his master. He nodded and smiled as, over and over, Monarch licked the hand of the one to whom he owed his very life. It was the same hand, in fact, that had reached out to him in far different circumstances.

Above all else, one thing stood out in the scene. It was obvious that Monarch had followed Jake into the room and had lain by his side out of sheer devotion. He didn't beg for food or whine for attention, but merely expressed gratitude for being able to rest in his master's presence. Looking up with eyes filled with rapt adoration and licking the hand of his master—the best way of expressing the love he felt— Monarch was content.[1]

We humans have a lot to learn from old Monarch. I do. He shows us how to worship! God longs for each of His children to express such love for Him. And why shouldn't we? Not one of us can ever come to our Master on our own terms. Or by our own merits. We have one claim to fame: without God, Satan's chains bind us tight around the post of sin. We deserve only the wrath of a holy, righteous God, but instead, He reaches down to us with His ultimate expression of love.

Monarch differs from most of us in that he knew his master had saved his life on that bitter winter night. His response in return? Showing his feelings of love without hesitation or reservation. Monarch's response is not mere fiction. Most dogs act the very same toward their owners. Consider the following true saga written long after Monarch's story.

Best-selling author and psychologist Dr. James Dobson, in his March, 1991, newsletter, tells about how the family acquired their new dog, Mitzi. While mourning the loss of Mindy, their twelve-year-old yellow Labrador, they began searching for another pet to fill the empty spot she left in their home. They scouted around the local animal shelter for the most pathetic, least likely adoption candidate— one nobody else would want. It wasn't a hard task.

A twelve-week-old semi-starved pup with pneumonia, a barely-healed broken jaw, and a bad case of worms trembled at the back of her cage. She stole their hearts with a single hug. Not too long afterward, the Dobsons' daughter went back to the shelter to pick her up. Dr. Dobson described their puppy one month later, "I wish you could see Mitzi today. She is fat, healthy and deliriously happy. When I get home at night, she romps to the front door like a buffalo in a stampede. It is as though she knows we rescued her from a living death."

Notice any similarities between Mitzi and Monarch? Besides their dismal pasts, I mean. Think about their love for their rescuers. Both dogs were so spontaneous. Uninhibited. Enthusiastic! We human beings find it far more difficult to adore our Master, who saved us. Worship often involves a life-long process of learning to simply let go. One popular worship song speaks of having a spirit set free for worship. I'm still in the process, believe me.

How do we cultivate an attitude of gratitude toward God? We'll cover that, so stay with me. By the last page, I believe you'll not only know how, but you will be doing it. Our goal as Christians should be to be more like Monarch and Mitzi and less like our natural selves—where our relationship to God is concerned, that is. We'll be addressing six major aspects of worship throughout the book (but not necessarily in this strict order).

1. *Who* we worship (Does He really deserve it?)
2. *What* worship is (And what it isn't)
3. *Where* we worship (Does it matter?)
4. *When* to worship (How about non-stop?)
5. *Why* we should worship (There are plenty of reasons)
6. *How* we worship (That's a hot topic!)

So let's begin by reminding ourselves why God created us in the first place. We have a deep, inner craving in us that He alone can fill. In fact, He created us to love Him.

> Now we were made to worship...All else fulfills its design;
> flowers are still fragrant and lilies are still beautiful and the
> bees still search for nectar amongst the flowers; the birds still
> sing with their thousand-voice choir on a summer's day, and
> the sun and the moon and the stars all move on their rounds
> doing the will of God.
>
> And from what we can learn from the Scriptures we
> believe that the seraphim and cherubim and powers and
> dominions are still fulfilling their design—worshiping God
> who also created them and breathed into them the breath of
> life. Man alone sulks in his cave. Man alone, with all of his
> brilliant intelligence, with all of his amazing, indescribable
> and wonderful equipment, still sulks in his cave.[2]

How few people understand and accept man's intrinsic need to worship God! Only as we acknowledge the emptiness that cries for worship can the constant unrest within us be settled. Our search for God will be most meaningful when we realize the utter barrenness of a soul separated from Him.

The void within us is spiritual, yet how often do we look to other areas of life in hope of finding the answer to our malaise? Everyone has heard stories of the busy executive, ruthlessly driven to success after success but who never achieves fulfillment. How about the "supermom" who loses herself in her children—only to feel devastated by loneliness when they grow up and move out on their own? More often than not, these unbalanced lifestyles stem from an unrecognized, or purposely avoided, spiritual longing. They want to love God but don't know it.

In varying degrees, most of us are probably guilty of seeking satisfaction through either intellectual, emotional, or physical stimulation. "Futility, futility, futility," moaned King Solomon after he had sampled every diversion known to man. It's an age-old problem. The glitter of Earth-bound methods loses its sparkle, leaving us disillusioned and depressed. (I ran down that dead-end street for years.) Sadly enough, even after many people know that the living God is the source of contentment, some still refuse to allow Him to do what He desires in their lives.

> There once was in man a true happiness of which now remains to him only the mark and empty trace, which he in vain tries to fill from all his surroundings, seeking from things absent the help he does not obtain in things present. But these are all inadequate, because the infinite abyss can only be filled by an infinite and immutable object, that is to say, only by God Himself.[3]

In our avoidance of God, we find ourselves surrounded by much company throughout history. When we look to the children of Israel as our spiritual predecessors, we see them running from their Creator at Mt. Sinai. After God freed His people from Egyptian slavery with one mighty miracle after another, He made them a most amazing offer. He asked them to enter into a personal relationship with Him. Listen to God's words to Moses (for him to pass on to the Israelites):

> "You yourselves have seen what I did to the Egyptians, and how I bore you on eagles' wings, and brought you to Myself. Now then, if you will indeed obey My voice and keep My covenant, then you shall be My own possession among all the peoples, for all the earth is Mine; and you shall be to Me a kingdom of priests and a holy nation." These are the words that you shall speak to the sons of Israel.
>
> —Exodus 19:4–6

Note the Israelites' enthusiastic response:

> All the people perceived the thunder and the lightning flashes and the sound of the trumpet and the mountain smoking; and when the people saw it, they trembled and stood at a distance. Then they said to Moses, "Speak to us yourself and we will listen; but let not God speak to us, or we will die." Moses said to the people, "Do not be afraid; for God has

come in order to test you, and in order that the fear of Him
may remain with you, so that you may not sin."
—EXODUS 20:18–20

The people failed to grasp the significance of God's invitation. He
was offering them the answer to their deep longing, but because of
fear and misunderstanding, they preferred to remain far from Him.

Centuries after the Mt. Sinai experience, neither the offer nor the
response had changed. Jesus was engaged in a candid yet compassionate conversation with a woman of Samaria. Alongside a well, He
was extending the wellspring of abundant life to her. He knew sexual
promiscuity could no more fill the needy vacuum within her than
could mere obedience of the Law for the Israelites. "No man can meet
a woman's spiritual needs, and a woman has not been born who can
meet a man's spiritual needs. Our spirit belongs to God and can only
find fulfillment and complete satisfaction in Him."[4]

The woman at the well failed to see her inner poverty and asked
Jesus, instead, about the proper place to worship. Wasn't she evading
the real issue—letting God get close to her? If we'll admit it, we run
from Him today just like she and the Israelites did. We do so in the
name of religion. Not worship.

Malcolm Smith, the British teacher, helps us smile at our ancestors'
standoffish attitude (and our own) in his excellent three-tape series
How to Rise Above Burnout.

> You understand why religion was invented. It was to keep
> God at a safe distance. I used to believe that all the religions
> of the world were men reaching out for God. It isn't. All the
> religions of the world are there to keep God at a safe distance.
> You see, man knows there's a God, but he's scared spitless of
> Him, so he's got to keep Him away.
>
> So I know what we'll do...we'll build a God-house and
> put Him in there! So we have the "house of God." That's got
> Him off my back. If He's in *His* house, He's not in mine!
> We'll give Him a certain day. That's it, we'll give Him one
> day. That gives me six.

I'll give Him times. We'll have hours of prayer. That means I won't have to pray all the time. Religion says, "Spend fifteen minutes in prayer every day." That gets Him off your back. Fifteen minutes. You've got the other twenty-three and three quarters. Right? Keep Him at a distance. See, I know He's there, but keep Him at a distance.

I tell you what we'll do...we'll employ people full-time to talk to Him. Then I don't have to, see. Religion. All religion is like that. I'm not joking. Religion keeps God at arm's length from man. And now religion is uneasy. Why? Because the God they're supposed to represent has *really* turned up among them. And they're very upset. God has escaped! He got out of the house! And He's walking among them, and He doesn't fit at all what they thought He was like.[5]

Genuine worship frees us from the bondage of preconceived notions and fake religion. Only as we worship, our spirits having been "released from captivity to soar in the presence of God" (Cornwall), can the "quiet desperation," as Thoreau called it, be relieved. No wonder Thoreau felt desperate. His writings express the humanistic belief in *selfhood* reigning supreme. (Nature is up there near the top of his list, too.) His ideas provided him no opportunity to worship Someone outside himself—the eternal Creator, the God of the Bible. Our answer to fulfillment lies not in man or in nature, which are both God's handiwork, but with the Lord of glory Himself. And in our worship of Him.

Worship is written upon the heart of man by the hand of God...In a broad sense, worship is inseparable from and is an expression of life. It is not that man cannot live without worship, it is that he cannot fully live without worship...man was made to worship as surely as he was made to breathe. We may restrict the expression of worship for a season, just as we may briefly hold our breath, but there is an inward craving for worship that cannot be permanently stilled.[6]

Even for the most dedicated Christian, today's world of push-button conveniences and fast food chains can be challenging to our spiritual priorities. Yet, we've got to get free of the influence of these easy-come, easy-go habits if we are to develop a balanced love relationship with God. There are no shortcuts that I know of, but I have found some keys that will unlock the door to true worship and kindle within each of us a heart aflame. We'll be exploring those ideas in more depth throughout this book.

How would you describe your own walk with God? Be honest with yourself. Could you say that you're enthusiastic? Alive and filled with His power? Are you consumed with zeal? Do you glow with a burning desire to please Him? Can you, like Monarch, rest contentedly in your Master's presence—and just enjoy being with Him? These questions measure the heart-fire of love. Perhaps the flame is but a dying ember at this point in your life—or has even gone out altogether. If so, you might consider a statement by the late A. W. Tozer: "Worship is the missing jewel of the evangelical church!"[7]

Many Christians have begun to discover the inadequacy of mere knowledge of God through His Word or even of their dedication to Him. They may have practiced both of these concepts from their youth, and yet, much to their dismay, admit that their hearts remain stone cold toward God. They don't love Him at all. Something is missing—the zeal, the passion that marks a true worshiper.

A mature relationship with the Lord embodies three components: *knowledge* of Him, *covenant* with Him, and *worship* of Him. These elements represent the complete love of God. If the relationship is to grow in a healthy manner, they must be present in equal measure. The three enhance one another in a kind of divine synergy. From worship comes an expansion of intimate knowledge and covenant, which in turn reinforces worship even further. Each element complements and completes the other two, but worship kindles the fire of passion for God (more about this in Chapter 2).

In my own personal search for worship, I attended many a Sunday service and crammed significant amounts of Bible verses into my head but failed to experience worship in my heart. Even in the Holy Land,

I found meaningful places to worship. Yet, I still lacked the ability to do so with any gusto or sincerity. Finally, in my attempts to catch this elusive butterfly, I realized that the fault lay not in the geographic location. The responsibility rested squarely in my lap. I had to admit to God and to myself that I really did not know *how* to worship. For years, I longed for the answer to this question to fill the hunger inside me. I searched in many ways, some a little unusual.

What is worship, anyway? I wondered. I had picked a difficult question because worship involves nearly every aspect of life.

As a starting point, we can investigate the Hebrew word *shachah*, translated "worship" in the Old Testament. It means "to prostrate (especially reflexive, in homage to royalty or God), bow (self) down, crouch, fall down (flat), humbly beseech, do (make) obeisance, do reverence, make to stoop, worship."[8] We worship something when we pay it great respect, considering it extremely precious and worthy of adoration. In the New Testament, the word for worship, *proskuneo,* means "to kiss the hand in token of reverence; by kneeling or prostration to do homage or make obeisance whether in order to express respect or to make supplication."[9]

Judson Cornwall draws a contrast between the meaning of the Old and New Testament words for worship. The two terms actually describe the difference between the old and new covenants. (Remember the Israelites cringing in fear at a safe distance from Mt. Sinai while Moses talked with God?) Judson makes it clear when he writes:

> The word "proskuneo" is far more descriptive than the Hebrew word "shachah," for to the bowing is added kissing, and this requires close contact. We can bow at a distance, but kissing requires contact.[10]

Webster's Dictionary sheds more light on the subject of worship: "to honor or reverence as a divine being or supernatural power; to regard with great or extravagant respect, honor, or devotion; to perform or take part in worship or an act of worship."[11]

These definitions address the external actions that may accompany worship, but speak little about what is actually taking place in the heart. A few other sources may help to broaden our understanding of this all-important activity. For example, "The chief end and duty of man is to glorify God and enjoy Him forever," states the Westminster Catechism. That sums up worship quite well. *Glorify. Enjoy.*

Someone else described worship as "a romance with God, an idealistic adventure of the extravagant and the mysterious in the spiritual realm." How poetic but true! In his writings, A. W. Tozer approached worship as "a feeling in the heart, expressed in an appropriate way." He also stated that the "soul of the worshiper should be the most godlike thing in the universe."[12]

William Temple, the late Archbishop of Canterbury, gave a beautiful description of worship in his book *The Hope of a New World:*

> To worship is to quicken the conscience by the holiness of God, to feed the mind with the truth of God, to purge the imagination by the beauty of God, to open the heart to the love of God, to devote the will to the purpose of God.[13]

Worship means to "practice the presence of God" in everything we do, every time we do it. Brother Lawrence, a seventeenth-century French Carmelite monk, wrote an entire book about the subject that has retained popularity until now. To practice the presence of God we must become intimately involved with the person of Jesus Christ. The special relationship and corresponding closeness that develop through the act of worship produce an obedience not possible in our own strength.

Granted, such lofty worship challenges us to the utmost, but the effect proves to be electrifying and fulfilling. That author I mentioned was right—worship is no less than a "romance" with God! All we need is a revelation of our Savior's mental and spiritual anxiety in Gethsemane, His fateful walk to Calvary, the agony He endured on the cross, and yet, His triumphant resurrection. One would think we'd shout, "Hallelujah! No wonder they call Him the Savior!" (The last sentence is the title of a fantastic book by Max Lucado.)

So worship, then, is a joining with and a rejoicing in all that God is, all that He's done, and all that He's yet to do. How can we fail to respond with grateful adoration? How can we sit on our hands? I don't know, but we do. Every day.

Worship consists of a feeling in the heart stemming from the "humbling but delightful sense of admiring awe and astonishing wonder of the God of the universe."[14] A worshiper experiences motivational feelings, and, yes, he has to express these feelings. Without emotion there can be no true worship.

But being an occasional worshiper "when the mood strikes" falls far short of attaining a lifestyle of worship—the key to spiritual transformation. The words of John MacArthur, Jr. speak volumes: "Worship is not merely an activity to be injected into our schedules at certain intervals; rather, worship is itself a whole-life commitment, an all-encompassing response to Holy God...."[15]

> If worship is love responding to love, and if nothing in heaven, on earth, or in hell can separate us from God's love, then surely nothing can separate us from responding to that love. That response is worship.[16]

FIRE-SEEKER'S COMPANION

Questions for Group Interaction or Individual Reflection

1. Compare and contrast yourself with Monarch and Mitzi. Do you really need and want profound changes in your life?

2. Why did God create you? Have you fulfilled that purpose? What effect has that had on you?

3. How have human beings responded to God over the centuries? Why?

4. Has the twenty-first-century lifestyle affected your ability to worship? How and why? What can you do about it?

5. What part does worship play in a balanced love of God? Name the other two important components.

6. Give as many definitions of *worship* as you can. Which mean the most to you? Why?

7. Why do you want to be a worshiper?

Open Sharing: Feel free to discuss questions or anything related to the chapter that ministered to members of the group. Let the Holy Spirit lead you.

Fire-Starter's Preparation

Spend time alone and together worshiping the Lord. Before and after, record your thoughts and feelings in a journal. Write down changes you notice in your life.

Notes

Chapter Two

A Delicate Balance

Knowledge. Covenant. Worship. Three vital elements that comprise an ideal relationship between creation and Creator. No one element carries more weight than either of the other two; rather, the three support one another in a beautiful symmetry. Three of anything means a good, solid amount. Some people say three is a perfect number, especially in light of the divine Trinity—Father, Son, and Holy Spirit. Out of twelve disciples, Jesus chose just three men—Peter, James, and John—to be closest to Him. After three days, He rose from the dead. Why not two days? Or four? We can't be sure. We only know He completed the Father's work in that time.

Three represents special strength. The Bible tells us in Ecclesiastes that a cord of three strands (symbolic of a marriage with Christ in the center) holds together best. Geometry teaches that a three-sided shape can endure stress more than other shapes. Hence, engineers often design bridges utilizing steel structures in a triangular pattern.

Have you ever heard about the main difference between two carbon compounds—diamonds and graphite (pencil lead)? Of course, everyone knows a diamond is the hardest stone while graphite is quite soft. The reason is this: in a diamond, the arrangement of carbon atoms forms a rigid, three-dimensional network instead of a flat plane! Recognizing, then, the "value of three" principle, let's take a look again at what I believe makes up an ideal relationship with God:

- Knowledge
- Covenant
- Worship

The symbol for such a perfect union? A triangle, of course!

As an aid to a better grasp of this concept of the human-divine relationship, we'll use an adaptation of psychologist Robert J. Sternberg's love triangles. He believes intimacy, commitment, and passion make up relationships between two people. We can expand that to knowledge, covenant, and worship in our relationship with God. The following illustrations show that it takes balance to achieve the highest possible love.

Every interaction that a person experiences has, to one degree or another, the following components: *emotional* (knowledge/ intimacy), *cognizant* (covenant/ commitment), and *motivational* (worship/ passion) factors. Each plays a vital part.

The outer triangle portrays the ideal balance between knowledge, covenant, and worship in a relationship with God, while the inner shows a corresponding balance between intimacy, commitment, and passion in a marital relationship, for example.

Harmony in either union should be our goal if we want to develop a healthy love that will grow, endure, and produce lasting fruit.

Let's look at the marriage triangle first. What do we mean by *intimacy*? Commitment? Passion?

Intimacy

On the emotional side of the love triangle lies intimacy, or "knowing"—a term that holds much more significance in the original biblical languages. In both Hebrew and Greek, "to know" implies an intimate relationship best seen in a very close friendship. To understand a spouse in this manner does not come easily. It takes time, effort, and the sharing of many different ideas and experiences. As one soul opens up to another, comradeship and mutual dependence lend support during times of trouble.

Many people who have been divorced, in looking back at the factors that may have led to their breakups, realize that emotional intimacy had diminished gradually as the years drifted by. They made the mistake of not pursuing a close friendship with their mates. As they grew in separate directions, they communicated less, shared fewer interests, and finally divorced with nothing in common.

Commitment

Now for the cognizant side of the love triangle. That's the "down-to-brass-tacks" loyalty in a marital relationship. It develops on more of a straightforward course than either intimacy or passion, and it provides the reliable strength necessary for the relationship to survive all the ups and downs of life.

Commitment will grow or wither depending on how it is nurtured. Each spouse makes a vow to do whatever possible to ensure the success of the marriage. That means total fidelity—no allowances for casual sexual encounters of any kind. What a solid foundation of trust that provides! Another classic example of commitment exists in the relationship between parent and child. Regardless of what the child does, the parents' commitment never falters. Well, almost never.

The following saying from a framed print hanging in our home describes this consistent quality better than I can.

Commitment is what transforms a promise into reality.
It is the words that speak boldly of your intentions
And the actions which speak louder than words.
It is making the time when there is none.
Coming through time after time, year after year after year.
Commitment is the stuff character is made of;
the power to change the face of things.
It is the daily triumph of integrity over skepticism.

—SARAH DOHERTY[1]

Passion

On the motivational side of the triangle we find the passion level in a relationship. Romance and physical union between husband and wife are essential components for fulfilling love. When they become one flesh in tender passion, their relationship embraces a uniqueness they have with no one else. Passion motivates them to greater commitment and leads to deeper intimacy between the partners. Passion cements the whole relationship into one cohesive bond. Trust grows during those moments, and they are able to express feelings otherwise unapproachable.

Marriages based entirely on the passionate aspect, however, often encounter difficulties that spell disaster. These relationships are characterized by numerous partners, varying interests, loose living, and consistently high rates of divorce. The volatile nature of passion causes "love" to flare up, but having no solid core, the relationship dies out.

A counterfeit of marital passion lies at the heart of those high-school crushes and childhood infatuations we've all experienced. Consider the schoolboy who "falls in love" with a beautiful girl in one of his classes. Although he thinks about her constantly, he never quite musters enough courage to introduce himself and get to know her better. Contrary to this, passion between spouses should be based on emotional intimacy, plus a devoted commitment that encourages them to hang in there when the going gets tough.

From the Human to the Divine

Ideally, every relationship would remain perfectly balanced. We live in a not-so-ideal world, however, with less-than-perfect human beings. Fortunately, we serve a perfect God who delights in a just balance.

By drawing a comparison between various interpersonal relationships and the human love of God, we'll be better able to understand the role of worship in spirituality. Intimacy/knowledge, commitment/covenant, and passion/worship will be present in varying degrees and change from time to time. In this section, we'll look at the off-balance combinations of these three elements that occur most often. An equilateral triangle (one with three equal sides) illustrates the model relationship. Scalene and isosceles triangles represent imbalances.

Acquaintances make up the majority of our interpersonal encounters. They exhibit a noticeable lack of any of the three elements of love, as shown by the dotted lines in the triangle. A man who commutes on a train to work every morning may exchange greetings and small talk with other commuters, but this is the extent of their relationship. Many people never develop more than casual acquaintances. At the root may lurk psychological problems, such as feelings of inferiority and fear of rejection.

How about someone acquainted with God? This person knows about the God of creation but certainly doesn't love Him. He and God have bumped into each other now and then. The person may have even joined a local church and sung hymns with the congregation, but he doesn't have a relationship with the Lord. His is merely an awareness of Someone he doesn't know on an intimate basis. There is no covenant and no worship, either.

Ice-Cold Relationships

Brrrr! This variation of human relationships boasts strong commitment but has so little intimacy and passion that it sends shivers down the spine. If marriage partners restrict the flow of genuine friendship and physical closeness between them, they end up with a relationship whose strength lies solely in the existence of the institution of marriage itself. It exists; therefore, it will continue to exist. The "until death do us part" flag flies alone at half-mast in bleak skies of marital unhappiness. Prearranged marriages often feel the chill, as well as unions where couples have thrown a wet blanket on the fire of passion.

In inspecting a cold relationship with God, we notice one important fact. Regardless of varying levels of knowledge and covenant, worship remains at an all-time low. Imbalance occurs for many reasons but

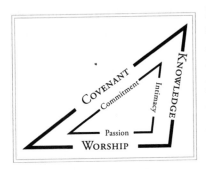

primarily because of cultural or doctrinal restraints. Far too common today is the frigid church that can't worship the God it serves. Even sadder is the church that once experienced glorious worship but has lost the ability to express love to God. Consider the Lord's words to the church at Ephesus, "But I have this against you, that you have left your first love" (Revelation 2:4).

A cold spiritual relationship may develop along several lines. The first example shows an abundance of covenant, some knowledge, and minimal worship. People here are often quite committed to the habit of their religion but don't really know what they believe or why they believe it. Strong commitment does have a benefit, however. These churches may have developed a ritual that will hold them together if all else fails. The trouble is, they mistake formalized behavior for true worship. In those cases where worship has declined to ritual, the Lord issues a stern warning. He will take away the light of His presence.

> Therefore remember from where you have fallen, and repent
> and do the deeds you did at first; or else I am coming to you

and will remove your lampstand out of its place—unless you repent.

—Revelation 2:5

The next example shows a better balance between knowledge and covenant, but still leaves worship at a minimum. God's heart of compassion has yet to thaw the ice enough to kindle in the churchgoers a heart aflame. They know what they should do based on the Word, and they're committed enough to try to act on that knowledge. Bible studies and service-oriented projects may even flourish in these cold churches, but without the fire of worship to give motivation and burn up impurities, judgmentalism and criticism tarnish relationships. Heartfelt joy is missing.

In the third cold variation upon a theme, knowledge has become the predominant factor. Intellectuals who study the Word of God but have less-than-optimum covenant and, again, minimal worship typify these chilly churches. For instance, cold Christians may look down on those who lack the same level of Bible knowledge or who fall short on memory verses.

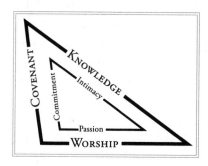

Chasing after the rabbit of knowledge for knowledge's sake alone leads right into the briar patch of legalism and self-righteous piety. Jesus often addressed two well-known religious groups, the Scribes and Pharisees. They had a corner on the religiosity market.

He showed disdain for their intellectual assent and external shows of obedience. "Whitewashed tombs," He called them and pointed out how they resembled persons who washed the outside of a cup and left the inside dirty (Matthew 23:27–28). The same goes for us. Without internal obedience of the heart encouraged through worship, the result may be a Christian who, in addition to being cold, is disobedient to God's laws.

Lukewarm Relationships

As comfortable as a pair of old kick-around shoes, the warm relationship between two people sports a high level of intimacy. For strength, this situation relies on shared emotional experiences and the results they produce. Daily routine and significant events, even tragic ones, bring about closeness and mutual acceptance that lend support to each spouse.

Warm mates exchange thoughts and ideas, and so improve their communication. They begin to know more about one another than anybody else. "Best buddies" we could call them—those who enjoy a companionship that endures even after physical attraction has faded. Passion plays an insignificant role in these relationships, often to the disappointment of one partner. Commitment may be present, and may even verge on unhealthy emotional codependency. They "need" each other's constant approval to feel good about themselves but at the same time take each other for granted. Mutual boredom puts them to sleep.

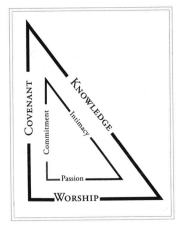

How about a warm love-of-God relationship with some Bible knowledge, some covenant, and a measure of worship? Christians in this category have been reading the Bible for a while and can recognize many verses but fail to grow in worship. They know God through His Word and may even have a degree of friendship with Him, but their hearts are not ablaze with zeal. His holy majesty doesn't faze them a whole lot.

They think they're on pretty good terms with "the Man upstairs" no matter how they act. It's a cozy situation for them, they feel. God's stern warning about lukewarm Christianity can light a fire under the complacent saint: "So because you are lukewarm, and neither hot nor cold, I will spit you out of My mouth" (Revelation 3:16).

Red-Hot Relationships

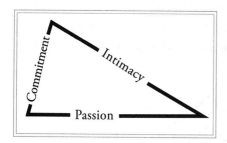

Hot relationships between people sizzle with passion. When passion as the strongest ingredient teams up with intimacy, a form of intense romantic love emerges. This "Romeo and Juliet" kind of love stirs up many young adults into a summer affair—until the first bout of disillusionment.

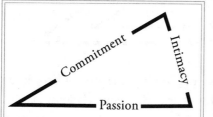

A second form of hot love occurs when passion and commitment are very strong, but intimacy is missing. Sternberg labeled this "Hollywood love." Here, the heat of fulfilling passion alone forges commitment, so the relationship lacks any emotional core necessary to endure the test of time.

Wild pendulum swings characterize hot relationships. The cycle begins on a very positive note and then veers in the opposite direction. This period of on-again, off-again, or hot-cold usually continues for a brief time. If it persists, it develops a highly negative factor. What began in the heat of passion winds up on the ice of contempt.

I don't intend to downgrade passion, by any means. Hugging, kissing, and making love within the bonds of marriage keep the home fires burning. In proper balance and at the appropriate time, physical affection enhances the desire for renewed commitment and even greater intimacy.

Hot relationships occur also in the love of God, with similar inherent weaknesses. Notice the example representing excessive worship with little emphasis placed on the Word—and the necessary obedience to it.

Christians who have this kind of relationship with the Lord go to church to experience an emotional high from congregational worship. If their private times with God don't include some fantastic supernatural visions as well, they think He has left them. They fail to recognize the volatility of trying to live from one "spiritual fix" to the next. Like any addiction, artificial worship creates an unhealthy dependence in the devotee.

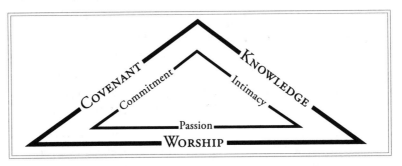

In another variation of the hot relationship, the level of knowledge approaches the degree of worship, but a covenant relationship with God has not been firmly established. Churches of this nature may experience glorious worship. Members love to chew on the meat of divine revelation from the pulpit instead of the spiritual baby food they think other Christians get. But they can't seem to make the transition from the mountaintop of academic knowledge to the trenches of dedicated service. During the heat of battle, they fall out, exhausted.

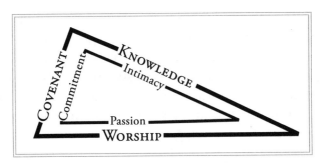

Without the deep commitment involved in covenant, endurance qualities of faith and trust become meaningless. When carried to extremes, lack of covenant may even lead to doubting the deity of God during rough times. Hot fellowships ride out many up-and-down swells in total membership rolls, and they hold a special attraction for Christians who have left other churches for one reason or another. Even in those cases of church growth explosion, a high rate of instability threatens to undermine progress.

Fired-up Christians who frequent these churches often exhibit a similar lack of commitment in their personal lives. When marital problems arise, they may be more apt to seek divorce. Their overall work and personal habits turn out to be far less than optimum. These vibrant, outgoing Christians know God and sincerely love to worship Him. Unfortunately, they fall short on a long-term commitment to obedience.

The third example of a hot relationship with God lacks knowledge. These churches, and the people who frequent them, have perhaps made a covenant with a God they love to worship. They just don't know Him very well yet.

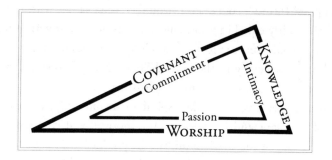

Because of their lack of knowledge of the Word, these Christians have a hard time sensing direction from the Holy Spirit of God. Their fervor to enjoy Him puts them in danger of being led astray. A Word deficiency may allow these zealous and hungry but uneducated Christians to wander along aberrant paths—even into cults.

Knowledge of God's Word maintains the accuracy of our worship, while covenant keeps us going over the long haul. All facets of the love relationship play a vital role. John Piper expressed this balance so well in his book *Desiring God.*

> Truth without emotion produces dead orthodoxy and a church full (or half-full) of artificial admirers (like people who write generic anniversary cards for a living). On the other hand, emotion without truth produces empty frenzy and cultivates shallow people who refuse the discipline of rigorous thought. But true worship comes from people who are deeply emotional and who love deep and sound doctrine. Strong affections for God rooted in truth are the bone and marrow of Biblical worship.[2]

Achieving and maintaining balance enables our love to evolve into all that God planned for us. Of supreme importance, of course, is the relationship we develop with the Father through Jesus Christ. Christian activity will only be as fulfilling and fruitful as the union we have with Jesus. We'll tackle that subject in the next few chapters.

Now mull over the late A. W. Tozer's famous statement again: "Worship is the missing jewel of the evangelical church." Which triangle best applies? (Hint: a cold one.) It would be the triangle with two long sides being fairly equal in knowledge and covenant, but with minimal worship. I would venture to say that chilly churches outnumber overheated ones, especially in the United States. Many people believe the lack of fervent worship has caused Christian churches everywhere to head into a dizzying downward spiral in membership, despite high levels of covenant and knowledge. The motivational component has been voted out of the curriculum by stuffy saints!

Maybe you, too, want to do something to help bring passionate worship back to the church. Stay with us for the rest of this book. Like enthusiastic diamond miners on an expedition to South Africa, let's set out in search of this precious gem. Once found, we can restore worship's rightful place—adorning the bride of Christ with sparkling beauty.

Balance is our goal!

FIRE-SEEKER'S COMPANION

Questions for Group Interaction or Individual Reflection

1. Name three key elements of a relationship between spouses and then between you and the Lord. Which element is cognizant, which emotional, which motivational? Draw a triangle representing the ideal, balanced relationship.

2. Think about the advantages and disadvantages of acquaintances versus relationships. Which do you have with your spouse (if you're married) and with the Lord? Why?

3. What three major "categories" of relationships did you study in this chapter? Where do you fit best as an individual? How about your church?

4. Talk about the characteristics of various "cold" relationships—human and divine. What dangers lie in these conditions? Draw triangles to represent them.

5. How about warm relationships? What advantages or disadvantages do you notice? Draw a triangle that indicates the imbalance.

6. Hot relationships come next. Describe them. Any cautions to watch out for? Draw the various triangles.

7. What similarities and differences do you see between marital relationships and a Christian's love for God? Explain.

Open Sharing: Feel free to discuss questions or anything related to the chapter that ministered to members of the group. Let the Holy Spirit lead you.

Fire-Starter's Preparation

Spend time alone and together worshiping the Lord. Before and after, record your thoughts and feelings in a journal. Write down changes you notice in your life.

Notes

_____

_____

_____

_____

_____

_____

_____

_____

_____

_____

_____

_____

_____

_____

_____

_____

_____

_____

_____

_____

_____

_____

Chapter Three

MAKING READY THE HEART

*When God measures a man, He puts a tape
around the heart instead of the head.*
AUTHOR UNKNOWN

REMEMBER HIGH SCHOOL days from years gone by? Maybe even university years? As you thumbed through the roster of classes, you may have stumbled on a subject that piqued your interest. "There it is!" you exclaimed. "That's the course I really want to take." But all too soon you noticed a tiny asterisk by the title. Down at the bottom of the page, you discovered that the asterisk indicated the need for a prerequisite—one or two other courses required first. Chances are good that you wouldn't have been equipped to absorb the subject matter, even if you had been able to finagle your way into the course.

In a similar way that schools lay down academic or *head* prerequisites, God has established some *heart* prerequisites before we can enjoy worship. First and foremost, only those who have been brought into a vital relationship with Him through Jesus Christ are capable of the kind of worship He has in mind. The unbeliever who has yet to be made new can't receive spiritual revelation. It sounds like foolishness. Nor can he worship God, no matter how hard he tries. Sin and self-consciousness obstruct his view. Jesus reminded the Pharisee Nicodemus, "Truly, truly, I say to you, unless one is born again he cannot see the kingdom of God" (John 3:3).

In fact, as Chuck Swindoll taught in a message on worship, "The only person *justified* in not worshiping is the unbeliever. For to worship you have to have a Savior, and your Savior has to be the central figure of your life" (emphasis added).[1]

For those of us who have entered into a Father-child relationship, God gives the divine directive to love Him. He said so in the first of the Ten Commandments (Exodus 20:3). Jesus underscored the same idea in the New Testament: "You shall love the LORD your God with all your heart, and with all your soul, and with all your mind. This is the great and foremost commandment" (Matthew 22:37–38).

Does this command imply a passionate expression of our knowledge of God? Is it a mandate for a burning dedication of our lives to Him above all else? Yes! To both of these questions—a resounding "Yes!" But we still face a choice. He always gives us the option. Once we've heard Him knocking on the door of our hearts, we decide whether or not to open up to Him, not only at the moment of new birth but throughout our growing relationship with Him.

> Behold, I stand at the door and knock; if anyone hears My voice and opens the door, I will come in to him and will dine with him, and he with Me.
>
> —REVELATION 3:20

By choosing to open up more and more of ourselves to close times with the Lord, we have made the most crucial decision ever. From this point on, every other choice in life presents either an obstacle or an opportunity for that relationship to grow. Major decisions related to a career, a mate, or a home are subject to other people. We actually have only one free choice—whether or not we'll worship the Lord. Sadly enough, most of us never even weigh the options. Other decisions take precedence, and we decide against worship by default.

The Divine Gardener cultivates the heart soil, breaking up the hard lumps of bad attitudes before we can ever begin to worship. God seeks humility in us. A humble heart comes supernaturally when we let go of our own willfulness—and with tremendous results.

> "Build up, build up, prepare the way, Remove every obstacle out of the way of My people." For thus says the high and exalted One Who lives forever, whose name is Holy, "I dwell on a high and holy place, And also with the contrite and lowly of spirit In order to revive the spirit of the lowly And to revive the heart of the contrite."
>
> —ISAIAH 57:14–15

Even Jesus humbled Himself. We have a hard time doing it, but He enables us to take on His thoughts and be broken before the Father.

> Have this attitude in yourselves which was also in Christ Jesus, who, although He existed in the form of God, did not regard equality with God a thing to be grasped, but emptied Himself, taking the form of a bond-servant, and being made in the likeness of men. Being found in appearance as a man, He humbled Himself by becoming obedient to the point of death, even death on a cross.
>
> —PHILIPPIANS 2:5–8

Mary of Bethany demonstrated a humble heart, which led her into a beautiful act of worship. We can read her story in John 12. She knelt down in front of a crowd of scoffing onlookers, anointed Jesus' feet with a pound of very expensive perfume, and wiped it away with her long hair. The whole room radiated with the glorious fragrance of her liberal gesture.

Mary's simple expression of love and gratitude to Jesus cost her about a year's earnings! Her heart was so completely "sold out" to the Savior that the cost of her gift didn't matter to her. She wanted no half-measures with which to express her devotion. She gave her best.

Lest we entertain the thought that worshiping is easy or that Christianity consists of singing a few songs on Sunday morning, A. P. Gibbs can set us straight with this comment: "The path of whole-hearted discipleship has never been crowded, or popular."[2]

As we embark on the road to becoming genuine worshipers, our actions will undoubtedly be as misunderstood, as were Mary's.

> But Judas Iscariot, one of His disciples, who was intending to betray Him, said, "Why was this perfume not sold for three hundred denarii, and given to poor people?"
>
> —JOHN 12:4–5

Judas reacted with his head instead of his heart. When we get criticized for our enthusiasm, we can take comfort from Jesus' reply to him: "Let her alone, so that she may keep it for the day of My burial. For you always have the poor with you, but you do not always have Me" (John 12:7–8).

Had Jesus' compassion for the poor run out? No. His whole life demonstrated His love for outcasts, and He commands us to help them, too. He was simply setting worship in its rightful place. Mary remained steadfast in her belief in Jesus as the Messiah in the face of the skepticism surrounding her. By her unreserved act of love, she would be the only one to hold the honor of having anointed Jesus for His burial. Can we, like Mary of Bethany, give our sacrificial best to Him?

Jesus Himself agonized and wept for the presence of God. Is it right to think that we can do any less? We must constantly hunger after God's presence, guard against becoming downcast or indifferent, and through it all, remain humble.

As we humble ourselves before God, we will in turn begin to see His greatness more and more, and vice versa. Finally, these two separate acts become one expression of worship. If we can but catch a tiny glimpse of our God as He truly is, our lives will gain eternal perspective. King David expresses both humility and awe in the psalms:

> O LORD, our Lord, How majestic is Your name in all the earth, Who have displayed Your splendor above the heavens!....When I consider Your heavens, the work of Your fingers, The moon and the stars, which You have ordained; What is man that You take thought of him, And the son of man that You care for him?
>
> —PSALM 8:1, 3–4

How we would like such worship to be natural for us, too! Only when we're humble can we fully appreciate the majesty of our God. Yet, at the same time, we can never achieve such a heart attitude of humility until we see the Lord as He really is. A divine revelation of the magnificence and absolute holiness of God causes healthy brokenness. Rather than causing us to draw back, cringing in fear, these qualities motivate us to worship Him with a passion. It may seem that we have reached an impasse with such apparent contradictions or antinomies. How can we be humble enough to see God without having seen Him, or to be broken and yet full of zeal?

What can we do to resolve this dilemma and begin to worship? In our own strength, nothing. Aside from being willing to grow into worshipers and to seek God with our whole hearts, genuine worship lies beyond our grasp. We can only wait upon God to supernaturally reveal Himself as He did with the prophet Isaiah. Notice, again, both humility and awe.

> I saw the Lord sitting on a throne, lofty and exalted, with the train of His robe filling the temple....Then I said, "Woe is me, for I am ruined! Because I am a man of unclean lips, And I live among a people of unclean lips; For my eyes have seen the King, the LORD of hosts."
>
> —ISAIAH 6:1, 5

Isaiah did more than sit on his hands and wait. Our waiting, like his, can be active, not passive. We can rest assured that as we turn our hearts fully toward God, He will reveal Himself so we can worship Him.

> You will seek Me and find Me when you search for Me with all your heart.
>
> —JEREMIAH 29:13

Time after time, the Scriptures reveal the Lord of glory through the eyes of Holy Spirit-inspired servants of old. As we delve into the Word's depths, we can cling to the fact that the same Spirit is waiting to lead us to a wealth of truth accessible only through Him. Why not, before continuing, ask the Holy Spirit to open the eyes of our understanding? We, too, want to discover (or rediscover) the glory of the one true God.

Questions for Group Interaction or Individual Reflection

1. How does enrolling in the "School of the Spirit" compare and contrast to taking academic classes?

2. Does everyone worship? Who can worship God? Why?

3. Is being a genuine worshiper easy? Why or why not? How do you feel about that?

4. What is the most important commandment in the Bible? How does it translate to everyday life in the twenty-first century?

5. Does God pressure us to worship? Why or why not? How does our decision to respond to God compare with other major decisions in life?

6. What qualities is God looking for in His worshipers? Does He really want us to "find" Him? Can we stir up in ourselves the ability to worship?

7. Name some biblical examples of genuine worshipers. Why do they qualify for such an esteemed position?

Open Sharing: Feel free to discuss questions or anything related to the chapter that ministered to members of the group. Let the Holy Spirit lead you.

FIRE-STARTER'S PREPARATION

Spend time alone and together worshiping the Lord. Before and after, record your thoughts and feelings in a journal. Write down changes you notice in your life.

NOTES

_____

_____

_____

_____

_____

_____

_____

_____

_____

_____

_____

_____

_____

_____

_____

_____

_____

_____

_____

_____

_____

_____

_____

PART II:

THE BLAZE BUILDS

Chapter Four

VISIONS OF GLORY

THINK ABOUT THE first time you took a family trip through beautiful countryside with a view so breathtaking that it roused "oohs" and "ahs" from everyone in the car. Waterfalls. Snow-covered peaks. Rolling hills resplendent with trees in hues of red, orange, yellow, and green. Meadows dotted with delicate wild-flowers. Waves crashing against a rocky coastline. You probably sat wide-eyed, trying to absorb every trace of beauty.

But suppose that same drive became your only route to work every day—to a job you didn't enjoy. Suppose you faced heavy traffic delays, no-passing curves, and a two-lane road full of potholes. Would the scenery be any less beautiful than the first time? Or would your ability to see grow dim?

So it is with our view of God. He is just as magnificent as He has been since eternity past. We're the ones who have grown bored, distracted, blasé. Or maybe our eyes have never really been opened to Him. Let's remove the veil obstructing our glimpse of Him as if we're wiping off layers of dirt from a masterpiece of art forgotten in an attic for years. Someone has said that we don't want for *wonders* around us, only *wonder*. King David never seemed to lose his childlike awe of God.

> Yours, O Lord, is the greatness and the power and the glory and the victory and the majesty, indeed everything that is in the heavens and the earth; Yours is the dominion, O Lord, and You exalt Yourself as head over all. Both riches and honor come from You, and You rule over all, and in Your hand is power and might; and it lies in Your hand to make great, and to strengthen everyone. Now therefore, our God, we thank You, and praise Your glorious name.
> —1 Chronicles 29:11–13

David, a "man after God's own heart," expressed true worship so well in those few lines. Through all the trials he had endured in his life, David came to know and appreciate the great God he served. Only from the lips of someone who loved God with all his heart could such freedom of speech flow. Consider these verses: "As the deer pants for the water brooks, So my soul pants for You, O God. My soul thirsts for God, for the living God" (Psalm 42:1–2).

We can better understand why David longed so for God when we catch a glimpse of three more visions of His glory, which He revealed centuries later to another saint, the apostle John. May God begin to develop within each one of us David's and John's same heart of love!

The apostle, while in exile on the isle of Patmos, received "pictures" of the Lord in His heavenly realm. John could see Him as he never had before—perhaps because he had no worldly distractions on that island. If we could ask John whether what he saw was worth being banished to such a solitary place, I would venture to say he'd exclaim, *"Oh, yes!"*

Immediately I was in the Spirit; and behold, a throne was
standing in heaven, and One sitting on the throne. And
He who was sitting was like a jasper stone and a sardius in
appearance; and there was rainbow around the throne, like
an emerald in appearance...Out from the throne come flashes
of lightning and sounds and peals of thunder. And there were
seven lamps of fire burning before the throne, which are the
seven Spirits of God.

—REVELATION 4:2–3, 5

No ordinary throne, this one, but the throne of the living God!
Exquisite colors, light, powerful sounds, and fire envelop Him. In the
next passage, God manifests Himself as the eternal Creator. He has
existed forever and will continue to exist. He created the universe and
its inhabitants for His own pleasure. So God has plenty of company
up there. Twenty-four elders and all the heavenly servants surround
His throne. What are they doing? Worshiping. God is so awesome,
they simply can't help but tell Him.

And day and night they do not cease to say, "Holy, Holy,
Holy, is the Lord God, the Almighty, who was and who is
and who is to come." And when the living creatures give
glory and honor and thanks to Him who sits on the throne,
to Him who lives forever and ever, the twenty-four elders
will fall down before Him who sits on the throne, and will
worship Him who lives forever and ever, and will cast their
crowns before the throne, saying, "Worthy are You, our Lord
and our God, to receive glory and honor and power; for You
created all things, and because of Your will they existed, and
were created."

—REVELATION 4:8–11

He is a holy God who always has and always will deserve glory
and honor. If He's worthy of nonstop adoration from all the hosts
of heaven, how much more should we, His children, worship Him
here on Earth? This scene points toward the first covenant with the

children of Israel and to the new covenant with the Gentiles. Many Bible scholars believe that twelve of the twenty-four elders are the patriarchs of the tribes of Israel. The other twelve may be the apostles of Jesus. The union of representatives from the old and new covenants indicates a turning point in God's relationship with man, and yet, His constancy.

As we read John's vision, we might notice that God is seated. He doesn't appear the least bit anxious about the direction things have taken in His creation. For those who fear, because of present circumstances, that God has lost control, this fact provides reassurance. We can draw much comfort in these troubled times. God reigns supreme. Everything proceeds according to His divine foreknowledge.

In the next celestial portrait, the hosts of heaven and Earth are worshiping God because He meets even the most crucial needs. As the drama first unfolded before John's eyes so long ago, he cried like a baby. No one in the universe was found worthy to open and read a very important book—the one with seven seals. An elder comforted him and then showed him more truth about Jesus, the man with whom John had spent three years.

> And one of the elders said to me, "Stop weeping; behold, the Lion that is from the tribe of Judah, the Root of David, has overcome so as to open the book and its seven seals." And I saw between the throne (with the four living creatures) and the elders a Lamb standing, as if slain, having seven horns and seven eyes, which are the seven Spirits of God, sent out into all the earth. And He came and took the book out of the right hand of Him who sat on the throne.
>
> —REVELATION 5:5–7

How did Jesus overcome? Why is He unique in worth, power, and position? Because the Father chose Him as His sacrificial Lamb—the only One perfect enough to give His life in exchange for humanity's sin. Jesus deserves our worship. Heaven's citizens certainly broke out singing over that fact.

> And they sang a new song, saying, "Worthy are You to
> take the book and to break its seals; for You were slain, and
> purchased for God with Your blood men from every tribe
> and tongue and people and nation."
>
> —REVELATION 5:9

At the close, John witnessed the most tremendous worship scene of
all time. Let's experience the wonder of it right along with him.

> Then I looked, and I heard the voice of many angels around
> the throne and the living creatures and the elders; and the
> number of them was myriads of myriads, and thousands of
> thousands, saying with a loud voice, "Worthy is the Lamb
> that was slain to receive power and riches and wisdom and
> might and honor and glory and blessing."
>
> —REVELATION 5:11–12

Picture yourself, for a moment, standing among the countless
multitudes as they join together to praise the One who gave His life
for His creation. How magnificent must be the sound of "thousands
of thousands" of voices raised to the glory of God! Could any of us
keep quiet on such a wondrous occasion? Our God reigns, and the
Lamb with Him!

God's superb plan also revealed to John a vivid contrast—Jesus
Christ as the mighty conquering King. This foreshadowed the second
coming of the Messiah, when He'll no longer be a meek Lamb. He
will come as a powerful ruler to claim His rightful inheritance.

> And I saw heaven opened, and behold, a white horse, and He
> who sat on it is called Faithful and True, and in righteousness
> He judges and wages war. His eyes are a flame of fire, and
> on His head are many diadems; and He has a name written
> on Him which no one knows except Himself. He is clothed
> with a robe dipped in blood, and His name is called The
> Word of God. And the armies which are in heaven, clothed
> in fine linen, white and clean, were following Him on white
> horses. From His mouth comes a sharp sword, so that with it

He may strike down the nations, and He will rule them with
a rod of iron; and He treads the wine press of the fierce wrath
of God, the Almighty. And on His robe and on His thigh He
has a name written, "King of kings, and Lord of lords."
                                        —REVELATION 19:11–16

Hallelujah! We can't mistake this message: Jesus stands alone as
King above all kings and Lord above all lords. He's set apart. Absolutely unique. When He returns with His army, He will enforce total
victory. We have this assurance from God Himself. The devil's time
of torment will come to an end; indeed, by faith, it has come to an
end already.

Isn't it plain why John saw God seated on the throne in sover-
eignty, not wringing His hands? Jesus will exact judgment upon those
who reject the free gift He offers. As the Living Word, He will judge
the world by the Word. Satan, the fallen angels, and those who have
been deceived will burn in the lake of fire forever—which leads us
to one more reason to worship God. We have been inducted into
the heavenly army to serve as priests and kings, and we'll escape this
everlasting death.

Yes, as the song goes, there is victory in Jesus! What the Father
began with creation, prophesied in the Old Testament, and fulfilled in
the New Testament, He will bring to a close when the King returns.
His ways are higher than our ways, and His thoughts higher than our
thoughts (Isaiah 55:9). We will not always understand what we see
happening around us, but if we keep our eyes on the Lord, we will be
able to say, "He's faithful. I know He is." God gives us the promise
in Romans 8:28 that eventually all things work into an overall plan
for good. For a season, that seems to be a lie. But how secure are His
promises? Can we really depend on His Word? He says we can.

For as the rain and the snow come down from heaven, And
do not return there without watering the earth, and making
it bear and sprout, And furnishing seed to the sower and
bread to the eater; So will My word be which goes forth from
My mouth; It will not return to Me empty, Without accom-

plishing what I desire, And without succeeding in the matter
for which I sent it.

—ISAIAH 55:10–11

Will we join with King David and John? How can we do anything
less than offer high praises to our God for such powerful promises?
Let's proclaim the glory of the Lord they loved. And we'll find more
reasons to worship after we learn more about Him in the next chapter.

FIRE-SEEKER'S COMPANION

Questions for Group Interaction or Individual Reflection

1. Has God become less awe-inspiring today than in biblical days? What causes a "ho-hum" attitude toward Him in your life?

2. Briefly explain what God showed John. Where was John at the time, and why do you suppose God showed him all that He did?

3. Describe the portrait John gives us of the Father. What position is He in, and what does that reveal about Him? How about the others present in the scene? Who are they, and what are they doing?

4. Why did John cry? Who and what comforted him? What is all the celebration about?

5. Compare and contrast the two glimpses John had of Jesus.

6. How can we be assured of God's dependability? What picture from nature does He use to remind us of this?

7. Can John's visions of God help you to worship Him better today? Why?

Open Sharing: Feel free to discuss questions or anything related to the chapter that ministered to members of the group. Let the Holy Spirit lead you.

Fire-Starter's Preparation

Spend time alone and together worshiping the Lord. Before and after, record your thoughts and feelings in a journal. Write down changes you notice in your life.

Notes

Chapter Five

GETTING TO KNOW HIM

N CHOOSING A life partner for marriage, wise singles want to be sure they know the person very well so that there is minimal guesswork. The checklist of a bride-to-be might read something like this: "How does he treat me and the people I care about? Does he love children? What are his values and goals? What kind of character does he show under stress? What has he accomplished in life up until now?" The more good traits, the better. The flower of love blooms in the light of desirable qualities. Until those spouses get a closer look— after marriage. Then they notice numerous flaws. Their partner leaves the cap off the toothpaste, throws dirty clothes in a heap on the floor, and spends too much money. Love can wither on the vine in a hurry.

But the more we know about God, the better He looks. We'll never discover any bad habits or shady traits about Him, no matter how deep we dig. We'll just find more evidence of His unique worth, of

His perfection—and our imperfections, which require Him to fill in the gaps.

In "Visions of Glory," we focused on the sublime, celestial side of God. We will see Him like that in heaven, but we can also know Him in a practical way now. Have you ever asked yourself the question, "Who is God, really?" What comes to mind when someone speaks of Jesus Christ? A random group of people asked these questions would no doubt give many descriptions, some of a sound scriptural basis and some otherwise.

A. W. Tozer has said that our most important thought is our conception of God. It should be as close as possible to the truth. Only then can we "worship Him in Spirit and in truth." It's critical that we grasp as much as we can about the One who created us, loved us, and died for us—the One who waits for the fulfillment of all things. John gave us a peek at the future, so let's gaze back at the past—which, of course, is all the same to God.

We can uncover a wealth of insight into the nature of God by looking at His different names. In the Hebrew language, a name held much more significance than names do in English today. A name expressed the nature, character, or purpose of the one to whom it referred. To pursue our understanding of who God is, we can best begin with how He revealed Himself to the children of Israel.

Elohim

We've all read or heard the first verse of the first chapter of the first book of the Bible, "God created." The word for "God" here is *Elohim*, and in it reside the first clues to God's identity. *Elohim*, a plural word, indicates His triune nature and His supremacy as the Creator. The One we worship is the eternal, immortal, invisible, the only wise God (1 Timothy 1:17). He is the Father, Son, and Holy Spirit, as well as our Father, our Lord, and the Spirit living in every believer.

> The worship of the eternal God through His eternal Spirit is far more than merely touching eternity; it is actually entering into an activity that is eternal in every dimension....

> Worshipers reach from before the world until after the world
> and join the angels of heaven in worship and adoration of
> God, "the Alpha and the Omega, the Beginning and the End,
> who is and who was and who is to come, the Almighty."[1]

In a memorable message on worship at a Fellowship of Christian
Athletes meeting, Anne Graham Lotz described God as being "Eternity, Divinity, and Activity." That sums up *Elohim* very well. God is
eternal and therefore not bound by the restrictions of time. He exists
outside of time itself. As the apostle Peter noted, a thousand years are
as one day in His sight. Space cannot bind Him, either. In His omnipresence and omniscience, He is present always and everywhere. He
sees and knows all things.

On only one occasion has God limited Himself to the boundaries
of time, and He did that for us! He chose to become a man. He
decided to take on the limitations of humanity by the Incarnation in
order to rescue it. When Jesus came in the flesh, He lived under the
same rules He expected man to obey. Then the Lord went one step
further. He submitted Himself to His own invention and allowed it
to crucify Him.

God expressed His divinity through creation, but He is much
greater than anything in it. He is set apart. *Elohim* created all and
controls all, yet He remains as separate from His creation as an artist
from his painting. A painting on canvas is but a reflection of the
artist, not the artist himself. So does the universe only reflect *Elohim*.

When we speak of the activity of God, we refer to the Creator as
we see Him in the opening chapters of Genesis and the first chapter
of John. Our Lord Jesus (the Word) certainly demonstrated an active
part of the Trinity.

> In the beginning was the Word, and the Word was with
> God, and the Word was God. He was in the beginning with
> God. All things came into being by Him, and apart from
> Him nothing came into being that has come into being.
> —JOHN 1:1–3

Let's worship Him, the eternal Creator, *Elohim*!

El Shaddai

This name appears in Genesis 17:1 as God's declaration to Abram. He said, "I am Almighty God [*El Shaddai*]." God's name combined His great and glorious nature (*El*) with His ability to provide (*Shaddai*). The meaning of *Shaddai* comes close to "a mother's breast."[2] In the same way that a mother's breast nourishes, comforts, and satisfies a helpless baby, our God nurtures us. In comparison to the vast universe, we are helpless.

We might note that only after God declared Himself as *El Shaddai* did He establish the covenant with Abram and change his name to Abraham. God was stating His intent and ability to fulfill His part in the relationship with Abraham and all of his descendants. Up until that time, people knew God as the Creator in an impersonal sort of way, but with this covenant, things changed. God unveiled a new revelation of His nature and a unique relationship began.

Let's worship Him, almighty God, *El Shaddai*!

Jehovah-Jireh

The meaning of *Jehovah-jireh* occurs in the passage where God commanded Abraham to offer his precious, long-awaited son as a sacrifice. The Lord required such obedience from Abraham as a means of testing or proving his faithfulness. Abraham needed to learn to trust God implicitly. Would God provide a means for his son, Isaac, to return with him from the mountain? Abraham believed so. His words to his servants even before climbing the mount of sacrifice showed his faith.

> On the third day Abraham raised his eyes and saw the place from a distance. Abraham said unto his young men, "Stay here with the donkey, and I and the lad will go over there; and we will worship and return to you."
>
> —GENESIS 22:4–5

Abraham's confidence in *Jehovah-jireh* never wavered. He may not have known the details of how Isaac would survive, but he knew that God would be faithful to His earlier promises. As we read further on, God demonstrated His undisputed authority. What did He require? Abraham's unquestioning obedience.

> Abraham stretched out his hand and took the knife to slay his son. But the angel of the LORD called to him from heaven and said, "Abraham, Abraham!" And he said, "Here I am." He said, "Do not stretch out your hand against the lad, and do nothing to him; for now I know that you fear God, since you have not withheld your son, your only son, from Me." Then Abraham raised his eyes and looked, and behold, behind him a ram caught in the thicket by his horns; and Abraham went and took the ram and offered him up for a burnt offering in the place of his son. Abraham called the name of that place [*Jehovah-jireh*] the LORD will Provide, as it is said to this day, "In the mount of the LORD it will be provided."
>
> —GENESIS 22:10–14

Abraham's tremendous act of faith foreshadowed the day when another Father would offer His only Son. Only He wouldn't spare His life—on purpose. Let's worship Him, the Lord our provider, *Jehovah-jireh*!

Jehovah-Nissi

This name means "the Lord our banner," the One high above us and around whom we rally in difficult times. He goes ahead of us in battle (spiritual or natural) so we know which direction to travel. When we look up at Him, He boosts our confidence and bolsters our courage so we can keep fighting to the end.

After their miraculous deliverance from Egypt, the children of Israel confronted the Amalekite tribe. In this first battle, God revealed Himself as *Jehovah-nissi* through Moses.

So Moses said to Joshua, "Choose men for us and go out, fight against Amalek. Tomorrow I will station myself on the top of the hill with the staff of God in my hand." Joshua did as Moses told him, and fought against Amalek; and Moses, Aaron, and Hur went up to the top of the hill. So it came about when Moses held his hand up, that Israel prevailed, and when he let his hand down, Amalek prevailed. But Moses' hands were heavy. Then they took a stone and put it under him, and he sat on it; and Aaron and Hur supported his hands, one on one side and one on the other. Thus his hands were steady until the sun set. So Joshua overwhelmed Amalek and his people with the edge of the sword. Then the LORD said to Moses, "Write this in a book as a memorial and recite it to Joshua, that I will utterly blot out the memory of Amalek from under heaven." Moses built an altar and named it [*Jehovah-nissi*] the LORD is My Banner.

—EXODUS 17:9–15

Each time Moses held up the rod of God, the people gained enough strength to overcome the enemy. When the rod came down, they lost ground. This rod provided a visible standard or ensign around which the people rallied, and when it remained high in the air, God performed feats of victory. Symbolic of God Himself, the rod pointed forward through the ages to Jesus. Like Moses, who built an altar to commemorate the Lord's name and His role in battle, we might remind ourselves often of the One high above us. We gather around *Jehovah-nissi* and exalt Him who "always leads us in triumph" (2 Corinthians 2:14).

Let's worship Him, the Lord our banner, *Jehovah-nissi*!

Jehovah-Rophe

After the children of Israel crossed the Red Sea by a mighty miracle, they languished in the wilderness without water for three days. When they finally found water, it was too bitter to drink. What disappointment! Once again, God proved He was truly their provider. Through the miraculous, He confirmed this new revelation of His nature as their healer, *Jehovah-rophe*.

> So the people grumbled at Moses, saying, "What shall we drink?" Then he cried out to the LORD, and the LORD showed him a tree; and he threw it into the waters, and the waters became sweet. There He made for them a statute and regulation, and there He tested them. And He said, "If you will give earnest heed to the voice of the LORD your God, and do what is right in His sight, and give ear to His commandments, and keep all His statutes, I will put none of the diseases on you which I have put on the Egyptians; for I, the LORD, am [*Jehovah-rophe*] your healer."
>
> —EXODUS 15:24–26

Let's worship Him, the Lord our healer, *Jehovah-rophe*!

Jehovah-Shalom

We could use a calming hand upon us during these troubled times, and the name *Jehovah-shalom* reveals Him as "the Lord our peace."

Gideon met God as *Jehovah-shalom* at a crucial point in his life and in history. The people of Israel were enduring extreme hardship under the oppressive power of the Midianites. They cried out for deliverance. God responded to their plea by sending an angel to tell Gideon that he had been chosen to be the instrument of their release.

Skepticism and fear gripped Gideon's heart. He didn't feel up to the dangerous task, and he reminded the Lord why. He came from the poorest, weakest clan, and he was the least among them, no less. That didn't bother God. He told Gideon that He would be with him. Gideon offered a present to the Lord of bread and meat and said he needed a more dramatic assurance of God's favor. He got it. With a touch of the angel's staff to the rock, fire sprang up and consumed Gideon's offering. But then he felt more afraid than ever.

> When Gideon saw that he was the angel of the LORD, he said, "Alas, O Lord GOD! For now I have seen the angel of

the LORD face to face." And the LORD said to him, "Peace to you, do not fear; you shall not die." Then Gideon built an altar there to the LORD and named it [*Jehovah-shalom*] the LORD is Peace.

—JUDGES 6:22–24

This revelation came at a time of national unrest and in the face of insurmountable odds. The same holds true for us today. No matter what circumstances we face—despite how things look or how we feel in the midst of turmoil—we have a wonderful assurance. Our peace does not depend upon anyone or anything. *God* is our peace.

Let's worship Him, the Lord our peace, *Jehovah-shalom*!

Jehovah-Tsidkenu

All our own righteous deeds are as filthy rags before a holy God, the Word reminds us in Isaiah 64:6. We need something outside ourselves to make us clean. God gave us this name, "the Lord our righteousness," in a prophetic word to Jeremiah.

"Behold, the days are coming," declares the LORD, "When I will raise up for David a righteous Branch; And He will reign as king and act wisely And do justice and righteousness in the land. In His days Judah will be saved, And Israel will dwell securely; And this is His name by which he will be called, [*Jehovah-tsidkenu*] The LORD our righteousness."

—JEREMIAH 23:5–6

Jehovah-tsidkenu points forward to the coming of Jesus as the perfect Lamb of God. We find in the writing of the apostle Paul that Jesus, who knew no sin, took on the burden of sin so that we might become the righteousness of God in Him (2 Corinthians 5:21). In a kind of divine exchange, we give Him our sin; He gives us His holiness. We turn in our old, dirty clothes; He dresses us in a brand new set of white garments.

Let's worship Him, the Lord our righteousness, *Jehovah-tsidkenu*!

Jehovah-M'kaddesh

Here we find another facet of God's nature, later manifested in the Son of God—*Jehovah-m'kaddesh*, the Lord our sanctifier. In addition to washing us clean inwardly (imparting to us His righteousness), He sets us apart as a unique, holy people of His own. His purposes become ours, and He uses us as He sees fit. In the Old Testament, keeping one day of the week as a special "Lord's day" provided an outward demonstration of His people's uniqueness. God gave the commandment to Moses:

> But as for you, speak to the sons of Israel, saying, "You shall surely observe My sabbaths; for this is a sign between Me and you throughout your generations, that you may know that I am [*Jehovah-m'kaddesh*] the LORD who sanctifies you."
> —EXODUS 31:13

How important that we realize our God sanctifies us, not we ourselves.

> Therefore Jesus also, that He might sanctify the people through His own blood.
> —HEBREWS 13:12

> Such were some of you; but you were washed, but you were sanctified, but you were justified in the name of the Lord Jesus Christ and in the Spirit of our God.
> —1 CORINTHIANS 6:11

We have only to accept what Jesus already accomplished on the cross. Then our habits outside will demonstrate to others what He has done for us inside.

Let's worship Him, the Lord our sanctifier, who distinguishes us from all others, *Jehovah-m'kaddesh*!

Jehovah-Shammah

God revealed Himself to Ezekiel as *Jehovah-shammah*, the One who is always present. The prophet had a vision of the Holy City the Lord will establish upon the new Earth at the close of the age. New Jerusalem will be God's dwelling place forever.

> The city shall be 18,000 cubits round about; and the name of the city from that day shall be [*Jehovah-shammah*] the LORD is there.
>
> —EZEKIEL 48:35

This passage does speak of a future event but applies to us today, as well. God still meets with man in His tabernacle, or temple. We, the members of His body, are living temples in which His Holy Spirit dwells (1 Corinthians 3:16). Jesus promised in Matthew 28:20, "Lo, I am with you always, even to the end of the age." On that glorious day we will walk the streets of New Jerusalem and see God face to face.

Let's worship Him, the Lord who is ever present with us, *Jehovah-shammah*!

Jehovah-Rohi

Almost everyone knows that beautiful psalm of King David: "The LORD is my shepherd, I shall not want" (Psalm 23:1). Jesus reminds us of the identity of the tenderhearted shepherd and how we can recognize Him in the following Scripture:

> I am the good shepherd: the good shepherd lays down His life for the sheep. He who is a hireling, and not a shepherd, who is not the owner of the sheep, beholds the wolf coming, and leaves the sheep, and flees, and the wolf snatches them, and scatters them.
>
> —JOHN 10:11–12

Without a leader to follow, we wander astray as easily as simple-minded sheep. They don't even know when they're lost. Our watchful, gentle Shepherd leads us to quiet waters of His Holy Spirit where we quench our thirst and to rich pastures of His Word where He guards us as we eat our fill. In that beautiful spot, He binds up our wounds and pursues us if we should wander off. He heals our broken hearts and leads us down paths of blessing because His name is at stake. When He makes a promise, He keeps it. Let's worship Him, our Good Shepherd, *Jehovah-rohi*!

Jehovah-Elyon

This name elevates God as the Lord Most High. There is none higher than He! For the Lord Most High is to be feared, a great King over all the Earth (Psalm 47:2).

> For Thou art the LORD Most High over all the earth; Thou art exalted far above all gods.
>
> —PSALM 97:9

Let's worship Him, the Lord Most High, *Jehovah-elyon*!

Jehovah-Hoseenu

Jehovah-hoseenu is the Lord our Maker, our personal Creator with whom we have a covenant relationship. This name acknowledges God as more than just the Creator of nature and other living things. He has a right to us, as well—our time, talent, treasure, and thoughts.

> Come, let us worship and bow down, Let us kneel before the LORD our Maker.
>
> —PSALM 95:6

Let's worship Him, the Lord our Maker, *Jehovah-hoseenu*!

Jehovah-Eloheenu

In this name, God declares Himself as the Lord our God. He is both Lord and a holy, set-apart God only to those of us who have entered into a covenant with Him.

> Exalt the LORD our God And worship at His footstool; Holy
> is He....O LORD our God, You answered them; You were
> a forgiving God to them, And yet an avenger of their evil
> deeds. Exalt the LORD our God and worship at His holy hill,
> For holy is the LORD our God.
>
> —PSALM 99:5, 8–9

Let's worship Him, the Lord our God, *Jehovah-eloheenu*!

Jehovah-Elohim

We find the first of many occurrences of this title, the Lord God, in
the second chapter of Genesis.

> These are the generations of the heavens and of the earth
> when they were created, in the day that the LORD God made
> the earth and the heavens.
>
> —GENESIS 2:4, KJV

This name, like others, proclaims the self-existent One, the eternal
Creator of all things, in covenant relationship with His people.

Let's worship Him, the Lord God, *Jehovah-elohim*!

Jehovah-Eloheka

When God gave Moses the Ten Commandments, He said He was
Jehovah-eloheka, Israel's Lord.

> I am the LORD your God, who brought you out of the land
> of Egypt, out of the house of slavery....You shall not worship
> them or serve them; for I, the LORD your God, am a jealous
> God....You shall not take the name of the LORD your God
> in vain.
>
> —EXODUS 20:2, 5, 7

Worship Him, spiritual Israel—the Lord your God, *Jehovah-eloheka*!

Jehovah-Elohay

God reveals Himself in even more of a personal relationship with His people. Each individual who knows Him can call Him "the Lord *my* God," the One who cares about me, no matter what events take place in the world. The prophet Zechariah referred to Him as such.

> Then the LORD, my God, will come, and all the holy ones with Him! In that day there will be no light; the luminaries will dwindle. For it will be a unique day which is known to the LORD, neither day nor night, but it will come about that at evening time there will be light....And the LORD will be king over all the earth; in that day the LORD will be the only one, and His name the only one.
>
> —ZECHARIAH 14:5–7, 9

Let each of us worship Him, the Lord my God, *Jehovah-elohay!*

Jehovah-Sabaoth

Perhaps the most famous passage in the Old Testament recounts the story of David and Goliath. It contains further revelation of God's character as *Jehovah-sabaoth*, the Lord of heaven's entire army of spiritual beings. You remember the scenario. An arrogant Philistine giant, Goliath, had been taunting the Israelite army over and over until finally a champion emerged—the young shepherd boy. But this unlikely warrior candidate knew his God. He had depended on Him when he faced wild animals that threatened his sheep. David ventured forth, not with the cumbersome, unfamiliar weapons of Saul's army but with his faithful staff and sling. Watch the thrilling encounter:

> The Philistine said to David, "Am I a dog, that you come to me with sticks?" And the Philistine cursed David by his gods. The Philistine also said to David, "Come to me, and I will give your flesh to the birds of the sky and the beasts of the field." Then David said to the Philistine, "You come to me with a sword, a spear, and a javelin, but I come to you in the

name of the LORD of hosts [*Jehovah-sabaoth*], the God of the
armies of Israel, whom you have taunted."

—1 SAMUEL 17:43–45

David charged and defeated Israel's intimidating enemy because he
knew the name of His power source. He advanced in the strength of
the God he served. We, too, can defeat every "giant" in the powerful
name of the Lord—by His authority.

Let's worship Him, the Lord of hosts, *Jehovah-sabaoth*!

Oh, yes, let's worship the One who can meet every single need. God
gave the *Jehovah* covenant names to the children of Israel, beginning
with Abraham. Gentile nations had accepted the idea of an eternal
Creator but did not know Him as their Lord and Master.

When He declared He was *Jehovah* (Lord) to Abraham, He formed
a special union with mankind. No longer could His own people
mistake Him for a distant Creator watching His creation from afar.
From that moment on He became Lord, Master, and King, who
would forever be personally involved with His subjects.

In that position, He promised to protect, to guide and direct, to
provide for, and to love His people as a father loves his children. This
relationship did not apply to all the inhabitants of the Earth, but only
to Abraham and his descendants who came to Him by faith. God
required something in return: love and obedience.

It may appear that the promises to the children of Israel have
no relevance for the Christian today. *Weren't the covenant names for
Abraham and his descendants?* you might wonder. Yes, but these promises still apply to us, too. We will see how this is possible, even though
most of us cannot call Abraham our ancestor.

Faith, the Word tells us, motivated Abraham to do all he did. Faith
in Jesus Christ enables humans to be born again. Ephesians 2:8–9
tells us, "For by grace you have been saved through faith; and that
not of yourselves, it is the gift of God." God becomes our Father, too,
because of all that Jesus Christ accomplished through His life, death,

and resurrection. By faith in what Jesus did, we become recipients of a heritage given only to the Jewish nation. What a fantastic truth! The apostle Paul explains this phenomenon further in his letter to the Galatians.

> The Scripture, foreseeing that God would justify the Gentiles by faith, preached the gospel beforehand to Abraham, saying, "All the nations shall be blessed in you." So then those who are of faith are blessed with Abraham, the believer....Christ redeemed us from the curse of the Law, having become a curse for us—for it is written, "Cursed is everyone who hangs on a tree"—in order that in Christ Jesus the blessing of Abraham might come to the Gentiles, so that we might receive the promise of the Spirit through faith....For you are all sons of God through faith in Christ Jesus....And if you belong to Christ, then you are Abraham's descendants, heirs according to promise.
>
> —GALATIANS 3:8–9, 13–14, 26, 29

To summarize then, who do we worship?

He is, first of all, *Elohim*, the eternal Creator who always was and always will be; and He is *El Shaddai*, our strength, the source of comfort, confidence, and nourishment. He is *Jehovah-jireh*, who has seen our needs and provided for them even before we know them, and *Jehovah-nissi*, the One who still calls us to rally around Him so He can perform miracles on our behalf. He is *Jehovah-rophe*, our kind Physician, and *Jehovah-shalom*, our peace in every situation, regardless of how circumstances may appear. *Jehovah-tsidkenu* gives us His righteousness in exchange for our sins, and *Jehovah-m'kaddesh* sets us apart for His purposes through His own precious blood. He is *Jehovah-shammah*, who is always present with us and in us, and *Jehovah-rohi*, the gentle Shepherd who leads us to quiet waters and green pastures. *Jehovah-elyon* is the Most High exalted above all, and *Jehovah-hoseenu* knows us even in our mother's womb. *Jehovah-eloheenu* is the Lord our God; *Jehovah-eloheka* is the Lord, Israel's God; and *Jehovah-elohay* is the Lord my God. Finally, He is *Jehovah-sabaoth*, the Lord of all the hosts of heaven and Earth.

Even though God has many different facets and a name for each of His characteristics, He remains a Trinity—Father, Son, and Holy Spirit. Here in the concept of the Trinity we find an antinomy. This, as we learned in an earlier chapter, consists of two ideas that appear contradictory, but are both true. In the divine Trinity, there are three who are God, and yet "the Lord our God is one" (Deuteronomy 6:4).

All true believers worship God the Father, the first person of the Trinity, because He desires worship.

> But an hour is coming, and now is, when the true worshipers will worship the Father in spirit and truth; for such people the Father seeks to be His worshipers.
>
> —JOHN 4:23

We worship our Father because He is the holy Father and the righteous Father (John 17:11, 25). He is the Father of glory (Ephesians 1:17) and the Father of light, from whom all good things come (James 1:17). He is the Father of mercies (2 Corinthians 1:3) and the Father of our Lord Jesus Christ (Ephesians 1:3; 1 Peter 1:3; and 2 John 3). Not only do we worship Him for who He is but for what He has done. Above all, the Father loves us very much.

> For God so loved the world, that he gave his only begotten Son, that whosoever believeth in him should not perish, but have everlasting life.
>
> —JOHN 3:16, KJV

> The Lord appeared to him from afar, saying, "I have loved you with an everlasting love; Therefore I have drawn you with lovingkindness."
>
> —JEREMIAH 31:3

He showed the depth of His love when He sent His own Son for us (1 John 4:9) that we might be sons of God (1 John 3:1). By the Father of our Lord we have been blessed with all spiritual blessings, chosen, predestined for adoption, made acceptable, redeemed, forgiven, and made aware of the mystery of His will (Ephesians 1:3–9). Finally, the Father has made it possible through His gift for us to enter into His presence to worship Him.

> Therefore, brethren, since we have confidence to enter the holy place by the blood of Jesus, by a new and living way which He inaugurated for us through the veil, that is, His flesh, and since we have a great priest over the house of God, let us draw near with a sincere heart in full assurance of faith, having our hearts sprinkled clean from an evil conscience and our bodies washed with pure water.
>
> —HEBREWS 10:19–22

Yes, the Father has prepared the way for us to worship Him through the Son, our Lord and Savior. Even the Son Himself proclaimed, "I am the way, the truth, and the life: no man cometh unto the Father, but by me" (John 14:6, KJV).

Calling God "Father" is a tremendous privilege. Did you know that one particular major world religion has almost one hundred names for their god, but "Father" doesn't show up once? That's because no path exists other than Jesus, the Word. We worship Jesus Christ, like the Father, for who He is, for what He has done, what He is doing, and for what He is yet to do.

Jesus, the Living Word, played a premier role in the creation of the universe.

> In the beginning was the Word, and the Word was with God, and the Word was God. He was in the beginning with God. All things came into being through Him, and apart from Him nothing came into being that has come into being.... And the Word became flesh, and dwelt among us, and we saw His glory, glory as of the only begotten from the Father, full of grace and truth.
>
> —JOHN 1:1–3, 14

> For by Him all things were created, both in the heavens and
> on earth, visible and invisible, whether thrones or dominions
> or rulers or authorities—all things have been created through
> Him and for Him.
>
> —COLOSSIANS 1:16

We find also that Jesus revealed the Father to the world. How? By taking on flesh and blood to walk among us. "No one has seen God at any time; the only begotten God who is in the bosom of the Father, He has explained Him" (John 1:18). "He who has seen Me has seen the Father," said Jesus (John 14:9). A child once said that Jesus came as "God with skin on." Christ became the fulfillment of the characteristics God communicated through His covenant names. In Jesus' own words:

> Now, Father, glorify Me together with Yourself, with the
> glory which I had with You before the world was. I have
> manifested Your name to the men whom You gave Me out
> of the world; they were Yours and You gave them to Me, and
> they have kept Your word.
>
> —JOHN 17:5–6

In the Old Testament, when Moses asked God His name, He replied, "I AM who I AM" (Exodus 3:14). Throughout the gospel of John, Jesus announced who He was in what some scholars have called the "I AM revelations." How similar in nature they are to the covenant names just studied! This is no coincidence, of course.

> I am the bread of life; he who comes to Me will not hunger,
> and he who believes in Me will never thirst.
>
> —JOHN 6:35

> I am the Light of the world; he who follows Me will not walk
> in the darkness, but will have the Light of life.
>
> —JOHN 8:12

I am the door; if anyone enters through Me, he will be saved, and will go in and out and find pasture.

—JOHN 10:9

I am the good shepherd; the good shepherd lays down His life for the sheep....I am the good shepherd, and I know My own, and My own know Me.

—JOHN 10:11, 14

I am the resurrection and the life; he who believes in Me will live even if he dies.

—JOHN 11:25

I am the way, and the truth, and the life; no one comes to the Father but through Me.

—JOHN 14:6

I am the true vine, and My Father is the vinedresser. Every branch in Me that does not bear fruit, He takes away; and every branch that bears fruit, He prunes it so that it may bear more fruit.

—JOHN 15:1–2

To all those who belong to Him, Jesus embodies every promise inherent in the Old Testament name *Jehovah*. Jesus not only provided food from heaven the way the Father sent manna in the wilderness; He is the Bread of Life that came down from above. He is the true Vine who always bears healthy fruit and the good Shepherd who gave His life for the sheep. We will never walk in darkness because He is the Light that disperses darkness. Jesus is the only way to the Father; in fact, He's the very door through which we enter. He died, but that marked a new beginning. He gives us true life because He rose from the dead and lives forevermore. He doesn't merely have life; He is life itself! Jesus, the man, was God incarnate. The prophet Isaiah foretold this centuries earlier.

> For a child will be born to us, a son will be given to us; And
> the government will rest on His shoulders; And His name
> will be called Wonderful Counselor, Mighty God, Eternal
> Father, Prince of Peace.
>
> —ISAIAH 9:6

As the Prince of Peace, He lived a holy life in perfect obedience to
His heavenly Father and finished the work He was given. After His
resurrection, Jesus ascended into heaven, where He now sits at the
right hand of the Father. There He presides as Head over the church.
At the end of the age, He will return to fulfill His promise to His
people.

> For the Lord Himself will descend from heaven with a shout,
> with the voice of the archangel and with the trumpet of God,
> and the dead in Christ will rise first. Then we who are alive
> and remain will be caught up together with them in the
> clouds to meet the Lord in the air, and so we shall always be
> with the Lord.
>
> —1 THESSALONIANS 4:16–17

Hallelujah! How can we keep from responding in worship and
adoration? Our future will make present suffering worth it. We serve
such a glorious God!

These passages have given us more insight into the nature of the
Father and the Son. What about the Holy Spirit, the third person
of the Trinity? In the Old Testament the word *ruach* is translated
into "spirit" 230 times. In the New Testament, the word *pneuma*
has a similar meaning. Both words imply an invisible force akin to
the breath of God. Yet He's a person. Through the Holy Spirit, God
communicates with us today.

Should we worship the Holy Spirit? The Word doesn't encourage
us to worship Him, although He is just as much God. The Spirit
Himself leads, instructs, and empowers us to worship. He guides us,

through the Word of God, to an ever-increasing appreciation of the Father and Son. A balanced diet of Scriptures and the Spirit makes the healthiest Christians. Most assuredly, the Holy Spirit will never persuade a believer to do anything contrary to the Word of God. He will lead the believer to a deeper and fuller revelation of the Divine.

Most Christians have read parts of the Bible. Yet, they admit they can't understand much of it—especially the more profound divine truths. Only the Holy Spirit can reveal the shades of meaning. Relying totally on His guidance, we submit our entire beings—spirits, souls, and bodies—to Him. That may take a while, because we cherish our independence. We surrender little by little. When we do, though, our study and prayer times as well as our praise and worship will produce much spiritual fruit.

As mere human beings, we simply don't know how to worship God. I told you how hard it's been for me. We, like the Israelites who danced around the golden calf, prefer to enjoy something we can see and *touch*. Yes, I know the Holy Spirit lives within every Christian, but only gradually do we learn to follow Him. Then we can worship in Spirit and in truth.

Many evangelical services and much contemporary Christian music cater only to man's emotions, which stem from the soul (intellect, will, and emotions) and not the spirit. In order for us to truly worship, or for that matter, to experience a genuine new birth and lasting transformation, our spirits must join with God's Spirit. Bob Mumford said it concisely: "When Spirit and spirit meet—there is worship!"[2]

God is love, Scripture informs us. Throughout the Bible, we see the Holy Spirit exhibiting the three characteristics that make up the love triangle. Not only do these elements comprise our love for Him but also they reflect His loving nature. He is the ultimate in knowledge, covenant, and worship. The same principle applies to the Father and Son, of course, because they are one God. For our purposes here, though, we'll look at the verses referring to the Holy Spirit.

He has knowledge and intelligence. We learn that He knows, speaks, intercedes, teaches, hears, and guides.

In the same way the Spirit also helps our weakness; for we do
not know how to pray as we should, but the Spirit Himself
intercedes for us with groanings too deep for words.

—ROMANS 8:26

But the Helper, the Holy Spirit, whom the Father will send
in My name, He will teach you all things, and bring to your
remembrance all that I said to you.

—JOHN 14:26

But when He, the Spirit of truth, comes, He will guide you
into all the truth; for He will not speak on His own initiative,
but whatever He hears, He will speak; and He will disclose to
you what is to come.

—JOHN 16:13

Does the Holy Spirit have a will and exhibit a covenant kind of
commitment toward us? Yes, for He struggles to bring our will under
submission and chastens us.

Then the Lord said, "My Spirit shall not strive with man
forever, because he also is flesh."

—GENESIS 6:3

For the flesh sets its desire against the Spirit, and the Spirit
against the flesh; for these are in opposition to one another,
so that you may not do the things that you please.

—GALATIANS 5:17

The Holy Spirit is motivated by strong passions, also, because we
know He was grieved and can be stifled or despised.

Do not grieve the Holy Spirit of God, by whom you were
sealed for the day of redemption.

—EPHESIANS 4:30

> Do not quench the Spirit.
>
> —1 Thessalonians 5:19

> How much severer punishment do you think he will deserve who has trampled under foot the Son of God, and has regarded as unclean the blood of the covenant by which he was sanctified, and has insulted the Spirit of grace?
>
> —Hebrews 10:29

The Holy Spirit has many titles in the Word of God, as well as many different abilities and functions. Above all, He is absolutely holy. He is the Spirit of truth and our Comforter. He is the Spirit of God, the Spirit of grace, the Spirit of Christ, the Spirit of glory, and the Spirit of promise.

During creation, the Holy Spirit brooded over the waters of the chaotic Earth. He inspired all Scripture (2 Timothy 3:16) and was present in Christ's incarnation (Luke 1:35), in Jesus' life on Earth (Matthew 3:16), and in His death. Through the power of the eternal Spirit, He offered Himself to the Father (Hebrews 9:14). In Jesus' post-resurrection ministry, "He had by the Holy Spirit given orders to the apostles" (Acts 1:2). Everywhere, we observe the Holy Spirit at work.

In the world, the Holy Spirit convicts man of sin and of his need for a Savior. Man recognizes his unrighteousness and his inability to meet God's requirements for holiness. Those who do accept Jesus' sacrifice as a gift are sealed with the Spirit until the day of redemption. This seal acts as a kind of down payment and assures us that God will fulfill all His promises. (Some of this information on the Trinity is from *Worship*, by A. P. Gibbs.[3])

How does He know our every need?

> For the eyes of the LORD move to and fro throughout the earth that He may strongly support those whose heart is completely His.
>
> —2 Chronicles 16:9

Behold, the eye of the LORD is on those who fear Him, On those who hope for His lovingkindness, To deliver their soul from death And to keep them alive in famine.

—PSALM 33:18–19

Our God, the omniscient, omnipresent, omnipotent One wants us to come to know the splendor of His majesty so we can worship Him—freely, joyfully, wholeheartedly. For, as John Piper said, "Worship is a way of gladly reflecting back to God the radiance of His worth."[4] In the next chapter, let's reach back thousands of years and discover more evidence in our case for worship. The findings may astound you.

Fire-Seeker's Companion

Questions for Group Interaction or Individual Reflection

1. Getting to know God is different from knowing anyone else. How? What does the name *Elohim* tell you about God? *El Shaddai* reveals a new facet of God in contrast with *Elohim*. Explain how this applies to you.

2. Who gave God the name *Jehovah-jireh?* Describe the circumstances and what that name means to you. Who named God *Jehovah-nissi*, and why? How does this affect your life?

3. *Jehovah-rophe* is another name for God. How did it come about? What does it say to you? Who gave God the name *Jehovah-shalom?* What led him to describe God this way? Does it apply to your circumstances?

4. *Jehovah-tsidkenu* means what? Who called God that and what was he prophesying with the name? What outward sign did God want from His people to show they knew Him as *Jehovah-m'kaddesh?* Is God saying anything to you through this name?

5. Who received the revelation of *Jehovah-shammah*, and under what circumstances? How does that affect you? What does *Jehovah-rohi* mean? Who called God that and what does that tell you about Him for today?

6. Describe the scene in which a servant of God named Him *Jehovah-sabaoth*. Apply that magnificent truth to your life right now. How does it make you feel?

7. In spite of God's many names, He is still one God, a Trinity. What is each member of the Trinity called? Name as many functions of each as you can. How do they interrelate?

Open Sharing: Feel free to discuss questions or anything related to the chapter that ministered to members of the group. Let the Holy Spirit lead you.

Fire-Starter's Preparation

Spend time alone and together worshiping the Lord. Before and after, record your thoughts and feelings in a journal. Write down changes you notice in your life.

Notes

Chapter Six

OF TABERNACLES AND TEMPLES

HAVE YOU EVER gone prospecting for gold? I haven't, either. But thousands of fortune hunters throughout history have abandoned homes and families, rushed to remote areas of the world, and risked life and limb—all in search of this cherished mineral. From what I've read, a prospector has to be quite patient and intent on striking genuine treasure. Why? Because the valuable mineral often comes attached to and buried under other less glamorous materials. Miners expend tremendous energy excavating tons of rock just to find a few ounces of gold. If prospectors go to major extremes to unearth a shiny metal, shouldn't we apprentice worshipers be willing to dig a little to discover valuable tidbits about God? No book on worship would be quite complete without a look at the setting for Old Testament worship. Many of us have missed precious gems in the Word by assuming that sections of the Old Testament contain an unending list of needless information. Although God's manner of dealing with man has changed somewhat throughout history, His principles remain unchanged by time.

How about if we approach the ancient tabernacle with the attitude of one seeking buried treasure? Even the minute details, in the way they foreshadow the Messiah, serve to confirm the perfection of God. The precise directions for the construction of the tabernacle in the wilderness, which God gave to Moses so many thousands of years ago, contain a wealth of information. Hidden in the tabernacle lie secrets of God's plan for man throughout the ages. We'll find insight as to how we, temples of the living God, should conduct ourselves as worshipers. John MacArthur, Jr. cautioned:

> Worship is not giddy. It does not rush into God's presence unprepared and insensitive to His majesty. It is not shallow, superficial, or flippant. Worship is life lived in the presence of an infinitely righteous and omnipresent God by one utterly aware of His holiness and consequently overwhelmed with his own unholiness.[1]

What does it mean to be "living temples"? The life-changing truths in the ancient tabernacle will help us to answer this question. As a springboard, we'll describe this old covenant place of worship. Each detail has special significance, so bear with us as we proceed slowly through this section.

The Lord called for the tabernacle of the congregation, or tent of meeting, to be situated in a strategic way among the twelve tribes. Numbers 2:2 records the precise order.

> The sons of Israel shall camp, each by his own standard, with the banners of their fathers' households; they shall camp around the tent of meeting at a distance.

God gave instructions for the tribes of Judah, Issachar, and Zebulun to camp on the east side; on the south side, the tribes of Reuben, Simeon, and Gad; on the west side, the tribes of Ephraim,

Manasseh, and Benjamin; while Dan, Asher, and Naphtali completed the arrangement on the north side. They erected the tabernacle, then, at the very center of the encampment. Only the sons of Aaron and the Levites, those set aside to minister to God, could set up camp near the tabernacle.

Like the hub of a wheel with spokes radiating outward, this tribal arrangement around the tabernacle made some dramatic statements: "Keep worship at the center of life! Revolve the rest of your life around it." That applies to us today, too. We often try to squeeze God into our schedules as an afterthought.

However, the Israelites had to place their personal tents far away from the tabernacle. The priests and Levites alone lived within a close proximity. This symbolized the covenant relationship that God established with His people for that period—He allowed only those in the priesthood to come into His presence.

Organizing the camp around the tabernacle offered another advantage. Everyone could see it with an unobstructed view whenever Moses went in to meet with God.

> And it came about, whenever Moses went out to the tent, that all the people would arise and stand, each at the entrance of his tent, and gaze after Moses until he entered the tent. Whenever Moses entered the tent, the pillar of cloud would descend and stand at the entrance of the tent; and the LORD would speak with Moses. When all the people saw the pillar of cloud standing at the entrance of the tent, all the people would arise and worship, each at the entrance of his tent.
>
> —EXODUS 33:8–10

When the pillar of cloud lifted, the Israelites could see a white linen fence-like enclosure and the badger skin covering the roof, visible above the fence. The only entrance opened into the east side of the outer fence. Over this gate hung curtains of blue, purple, scarlet, and white linen. Passing through the gate and entering the courtyard, they encountered three distinct objects: the laver, the brazen altar, and the tabernacle itself. Before entering the house of God, the priests washed in the laver, a large brass basin located just outside the door of the tabernacle.

> Aaron and his sons shall wash their hands and their feet from it; when they enter the tent of meeting, they shall wash with water, so that they will not die; or when they approach the altar to minister, by offering up in smoke a fire sacrifice to the LORD. So they shall wash their hands and their feet, so that they will not die; and it shall be a perpetual statute for them, for Aaron and his descendants throughout their generations.
>
> —EXODUS 30:19–21

Adjacent to the laver stood the altar of sacrifice. As we just read, the priests had to be clean before they could offer any sacrifices. The penalty for failing to obey? Death. Both the altar and the laver were constructed of brass—the laver was solid, while the altar was made of shittim wood overlaid with brass.

Four distinct layers of materials formed a tent-like roof on the tabernacle. Its innermost layer consisted of curtains of fine white linen as well as blue, purple, and scarlet. Eleven curtains of goat hair covered this multicolored fabric. The next layer was a covering of ram skin dyed red and finally an outer covering of plain badger skin. Craftsmen made the walls of shittim wood and overlaid it with gold on the side facing inward. The door was made of hangings of white, blue, purple, and scarlet, supported by five shittim wood posts overlaid with gold and sitting on a base of brass.

Just inside the tabernacle in the holy place were three objects: one directly ahead, one to the left, and one to the right. On the left stood a candlestick made of one solid piece of beaten gold, from which emanated all the light in the holy place.

> Then you shall make a lampstand of pure gold. The lampstand and its base and its shaft are to be made of hammered work; its cups, its bulbs and its flowers shall be of one piece with it. Six branches shall go out from its sides; three branches of the lampstand from its one side and three

branches of the lampstand from its other side....Then you shall make its lamps seven in number; and they shall mount its lamps so as to shed light on the space in front of it.

—Exodus 25:31–32, 37

On the right side of the room was the second object, the table of showbread constructed of shittim wood overlaid with pure gold. The priests kept bread on it continually before the Lord. The third object in the holy place was the altar of incense, again of shittim wood covered with pure gold. On this altar, the priests burned special incense each morning as a sweet smell unto the Lord.

Directly behind the altar of incense hung a veil that separated the holy place from the most holy place (the holy of holies). The same four colors used in other curtains (blue, purple, scarlet, and white), comprised this veil. In the most holy place, the priest placed a solitary object, the ark of the covenant. Constructed also of shittim wood covered inside and out with pure gold, the ark looked like a gleaming chest. On top of the ark was the mercy seat, made of one solid piece of pure gold. Two cherubim with their wings outstretched and their faces looking toward one another stood on the mercy seat.

That completes our brief "tour" of the tabernacle. Didn't God lay out precise instructions for the children of Israel to build a meeting place for Him? Let's take a closer look at the rich symbolism.

Each of the four colors in the curtains and wall hangings highlighted a specific aspect of the character and work of Jesus. White symbolized purity. It pointed toward the holy life He lived as the God-man on Earth. Blue announced Jesus as the High Priest, and purple testified of His kingship. The fourth color, scarlet, revealed Him as the suffering Savior.

From the symbolism of these four colors, we can see why the color white made up the outer enclosure. If anyone would gaze at the visible characteristics and behavior of Jesus, they could appreciate His very human yet perfect life. Absolute purity distinguished Him from every other human being. Yet, worshipers may follow in His footsteps by depending on His Spirit. Qualities of purity and holiness in us draw people to Jesus.

What lay beyond the white enclosure, unnoticeable from a casual glance, spoke of a miracle: *Emmanuel*. God with us. An Israelite who approached the tabernacle would come upon a gate of multicolored curtains. It represented the Lord Jesus as the only way into God's presence. Remember His own Words, "I am the Way, and the Truth, and the Life," and "I am the Door of the sheep." We pass through this gate, in essence, when we accept Him as our personal Shepherd and Savior.

Being born again releases a supernatural joy into our lives. Delivered from the destruction of sin to the solid rock of faith, we can rejoice just like King David. He so relished God's presence, he said he would rather spend one day in the courtyard than a thousand days outside (Psalm 84:10).

For a Christian, life within the enclosure of the "courtyard" takes on new meaning from life without. Joy permeates seven commands essential to the life of the newborn worshiper. Since we are only just beginning to unravel the symbolism of the tabernacle, let's look at Psalm 100, which sheds more light on the role of praise, the predecessor to worship in the holy of holies.

1. Shout joyfully

2. Serve with gladness

3. Come with joyful singing

4. Know our God who made us

5. Enter His gates with thanksgiving

6. Enter His courts with praise

7. Give thanks and bless His name

Why? "For the LORD is good; His lovingkindness is everlasting And His faithfulness to all generations" (Psalm 100:5).

The first two commands characterize our daily walk with the Lord—to let everyone see our joy and willingness to serve Him. Singing, the third command, prepares us to come before the Lord in worship. The Israelites did this as they went to the tabernacle in the wilderness and later as they went to the temple in Jerusalem. Along the way, they praised God on instruments and with uplifted voices.

Once at the place of worship, the next two commands come into play. We need a reminder of who we're worshiping: Father and Son in all their wondrous glory. God is our Maker; we are His. Next, the psalmist urges us again to come singing our thanks and praise. The seventh command is to be grateful for having been in the presence of our God and to bless His name because of His great goodness.

These seven commands pertain to us today as much as to the Hebrews—even more so now that we have become living temples. At the moment we accept Jesus as Lord and Savior, we pass from death to life, and as we mentioned, symbolically we move into the outer enclosure. However, many Christians remain in the courtyard for the rest of their lives. Satisfied and smug with salvation, they fail to pursue God fervently enough to enter the holy place and ultimately the holy of holies. Since the Lord has allowed us even to enter the courtyard, we have plenty of reasons to be full of jubilant praise and thanksgiving.

These acts of obedience will lead us on to the lifestyle of true worship we desire. In fact, praise is such an important preface to worship that we'll include one more song by the "sweet psalmist of Israel." Psalm 150 begins and ends with the command to praise and in between tells us where, why, how, and who should praise the Lord.

Praise the LORD!
Praise God in His sanctuary;
Praise Him in His mighty expanse.
Praise Him for His mighty deeds;
Praise Him according to His excellent greatness.
Praise Him with trumpet sound;
Praise Him with harp and lyre.
Praise Him with timbrel and dancing;
Praise Him with stringed instruments and pipe.
Praise Him with loud cymbals;
Praise Him with resounding cymbals.

Let everything that has breath praise the LORD.
Praise the LORD!

Now back to the rest of the ancient tabernacle. Having entered the gate, the priests stopped next at the laver. When they washed their hands and feet in that basin of highly polished brass, they saw the reflection of their faces.

> And he made the laver of brass, and the foot of it brass, of the lookingglasses of the women assembling, which assembled at the door of the tabernacle of the congregation.
>
> —EXODUS 38:8, KJV

The laver is a symbol of the Word of God, compared to a mirror in the book of James.

> For if anyone is a hearer of the word and not a doer, he is like a man who looks at his natural face in a mirror; for once he has looked at himself and gone away, he has immediately forgotten what kind of person he was.
>
> —JAMES 1:23–24

The laver had a dual purpose. According to Judson Cornwall, it "offered a place of both self-inspection and self-purification, for the same basin that revealed defilement afforded the means to remove that contamination."[2] So does the Word of God! From the book of Ephesians we learn that the Word washes us, just as the priests washed themselves in the laver.

> That He might sanctify her, having cleansed her by the washing of water with the word, that He might present to Himself the church in all her glory, having no spot or wrinkle or any such thing; but that she would be holy and blameless.
>
> —EPHESIANS 5:26–27

Through a daily application of the Word to our lives, the Lord cleanses us from the ways of the world. As we let Him give us a good scrub, He will lead us to the next step—the brazen altar. The significance of the sacrificial altar can only be found in the Word, which explains why the laver came first in the tabernacle. Jewish priests placed offerings on the altar every morning and evening. These offerings foreshadowed the death of Jesus, the Lamb of God. They are also symbolic of God's requirements in each of our lives. A further study of the offerings and sacrifices will equip us with some useful insight as to what Jesus accomplished on the cross, as well as God's provision for us to enter His presence in worship.

The following valuable summary provides a key to the meaning of five separate offerings described in the book of Leviticus.

- Burnt offering: *surrender* of Christ for the world
- Meal offering: *service* of Christ in life
- Peace offering: *serenity* of Christ in life
- Sin offering: *substitute* of Christ for sin
- Trespass offering: *satisfaction* of Christ for demands of God[3]

In preparation for the Old Testament burnt offering, priests had to slaughter a healthy animal, sprinkle its blood on and around the altar, and then let the fire totally consume it as "a burnt sacrifice, an offering made by fire, of a sweet savour unto the LORD" (Leviticus 1:17, KJV). The burnt or ascending offering symbolized Jesus' willingness to lay down His life as the perfect sacrificial Lamb for the redemption of a lost world.

We also see the necessity of our acceptance of His act of love, as well as a total consecration of our lives to Him. Our act of surrender needs to be as voluntary as the Lord's. We offer ourselves to Him at the moment of salvation and every day thereafter for the rest of our lives. As true worshipers, we dedicate ourselves to Him without compromise. Just as the offering on the brazen altar was consumed by fire, so does the Lord long to see our hearts passionately consumed with the fire of love for Him.

The meal or grain offering was symbolic of the way Christ gave

Himself to the Father for the service of man. We can see this in the
description of the offering.

> Now when anyone presents a grain offering as an offering to
> the LORD, his offering shall be of fine flour, and he shall pour
> oil on it and put frankincense on it...And the priest shall
> offer it up in smoke as its memorial portion on the altar, an
> offering by fire of a soothing aroma to the LORD.
>
> —LEVITICUS 2:1–2

Here, the use of fine flour symbolized Jesus as the Bread of Life,
untainted with sin, who had the fullness of the Holy Spirit (oil)
poured out upon Him. Frankincense had a bitter taste but a beautiful scent when burned. This was prophetic, giving us insight into
the bitter agony and humiliation that Jesus would endure, as well as
how His uncompromising obedience would please the Father. Why?
Because of the results.

Peace offerings, also called fellowship offerings, had their own
special purpose, and they mean something for us, as well.

First, read part of the formalities:

> Now if His offering is a sacrifice of peace offerings, if he is
> going to offer out of the herd, whether male or female, he
> shall offer it without defect before the LORD....Then Aaron's
> sons shall offer it up in smoke on the altar on the burnt
> offering, which is on the wood that is on the fire; it is an
> offering by fire of a soothing aroma to the LORD....Now as
> for the flesh of the sacrifice of his thanksgiving peace offer-
> ings, it shall be eaten on the day of his offering.
>
> —LEVITICUS 3:1, 5; 7:15

A peace offering differed from others in that it couldn't stand
alone. Notice how the priests had instructions to place it on the burnt
offering instead of directly on the wood on the altar. That could be
because peace offerings symbolized restored fellowship with God
made possible for us only by the atoning sacrifice of Jesus. No accept-

able sacrifice first, no peace. Hebrews could eat the offering in joyful celebration of forgiveness and renewed closeness with God. We can celebrate, too!

The priests performed the sin offering every time someone unintentionally broke one of God's laws.

> If a person sins unintentionally in any of the things which the LORD has commanded not to be done, and commits any of them, if the anointed priest sins so as to bring guilt on the people, then let him offer to the LORD a bull without defect.
> —LEVITICUS 4:2–3

The animal was killed in the same manner as the other offerings, but the priest only dipped one finger in the blood and then sprinkled it seven times in front of the veil of the sanctuary before he poured the rest of the blood around the altar. This act foreshadowed Jesus' substitutionary sacrifice for the sins of mankind through the crucifixion, as well as the power of the Lamb's blood as the only means of cleansing humanity from sin forever. Each of us needs forgiveness. Inherent in a few drops of Jesus' blood is enough power to grant that forgiveness and open the way for all believers to enter into God's presence.

The fifth offering, the trespass (guilt) offering, covered any sin against the Lord's holy things. In addition to the animal sacrifice, the offender paid a sum of money to the one who was offended or injured.

> If a person acts unfaithfully and sins unintentionally against the LORD's holy things, then he shall bring his guilt offering to the LORD: a ram without defect from the flock, according to your valuation in silver by shekels, in terms of the shekel of the sanctuary, for a guilt offering...and it will be forgiven him.
> —LEVITICUS 5:15–16

Jesus removed our guilt before a holy Father, for He is the One we offend by our sin. Even the unintentional variety is serious enough to have required an offering to atone for it in the Old Testament. Some people think they're not guilty of anything because they, unlike criminals, have never purposely done wrong, but this passage makes it clear that any sin is serious. The blood of Jesus not only takes away our guilt before the Father, it also eliminates constant feelings of guilt, which hinder fellowship.

Offerings played an important role in the everyday activities of Old Testament Jews. Through such strict customs, they came to understand a recurring theme: *they could not purify themselves before God.* It took the shedding of blood from something apart from themselves. The need for animal sacrifices and offerings have passed away since the death of Jesus, but the underlying principle has not. A study of ancient offerings can lead us to appreciate more the costliness of sin and the tremendous penalty the Son of God already paid on our behalf. Sin bears a heavy price! It cost Jesus His very life.

Our own worship and offerings should cost us something, too. If they don't, are they really sacrifices? We're not implying we must work or punish ourselves so our sins can be forgiven. Jesus fulfilled this requirement once and for all by giving His life on the Cross. Only through the blood of Jesus (brazen altar), as revealed through the Word (laver), do we have access to the presence of God. If we accept this and follow in His footsteps of our own free will, we can pick up our crosses daily. Every fleshly desire gets crucified.

> I urge you, Therefore, brethren, by the mercies of God, to present your bodies a living and holy sacrifice, acceptable to God, which is your spiritual service of worship.
>
> —ROMANS 12:1

Once the offerings were completed, the Israelite priest would be standing outside the door of the tabernacle itself. Before we enter, let's look at what the outside of the tabernacle had to say. The curtains of four colors again foretold Jesus in all His glory: perfect Man, Priest, King, and Savior.

Covering the beautiful, colored curtains were more curtains of woven goats' hair. As one can imagine, they would be rough-textured even after being woven together. This was symbolic of the lifestyle of

Jesus. Rather than the pampered, genteel existence of kingly courts, He had the rough, earthy life of a carpenter and traveling preacher.

In the ram skin dyed red resided the revelation of Jesus as the sacrificial Lamb. Badger skin as the outer covering pointed toward the portrait the prophet Isaiah would paint of Him.

> He has no stately form or majesty That we should look upon Him, Nor appearance that we should be attracted to Him. He was despised and forsaken of men, A man of sorrows and acquainted with grief; And like one from whom men hide their face He was despised, and we did not esteem Him.
>
> —ISAIAH 53:2–3

After enduring beating and whipping, then hanging on a cross to die slowly, Jesus' outward appearance must have been pretty awful. The truth of His glorious identity remained hidden beneath an unappealing exterior. Similarly, the ugly badger skin covering the tabernacle completely disguised the glory of the presence of God within.

Thus far, we've met Jesus as the perfect Man (outer enclosure) and the suffering Savior (brazen altar). If we are to come to know Him intimately as our High Priest and King, we must take the next step. The door of the tabernacle differed from the gate in the outer enclosure. Five posts instead of four supported this opening, symbolizing the five-fold ministry that began with the infilling of the Holy Spirit on the day of Pentecost. The ministries of the apostle, prophet, evangelist, pastor, and teacher lead us through the door and on to a deeper revelation of Jesus.

Pure gold covered the five posts, speaking of the purity that must be present in the lives of these servants. Brass bases indicate that they must be tried by the fire of suffering before they can lead. After God has proven and anointed them, they have the ability to bring people into His presence.

Inside the holy place, one would come upon an awesome sight—wall-to-wall gold. This revealed the radiant purity of Jesus, as well the need for purity in the life of a worshiper. There in the holy place, only the golden lampstand with its seven lamps shed any light in the room. The source of light, the lampstand, symbolized our Lord, anointed with the fullness of the Holy Spirit, and the lamps represented seven attributes of that Spirit.

> The Spirit of the LORD will rest on Him, The spirit of wisdom and understanding, the spirit of counsel and strength, The spirit of knowledge and the fear of the LORD.
>
> —ISAIAH 11:2

Craftsmen hammered the lampstand into the proper shape from one solid piece of gold, and only pure, beaten olive oil could burn in it. Every morning and evening, the priests cleaned and trimmed the lamps' wicks and added fresh oil to insure that the light would burn continually.

In this description, we find some clues that tell us how to become better vessels of the Spirit of God. Both the gold for the candlestick and the olive oil had to undergo some changes before they could produce light. Likewise, we surrender and let God mold us into shape, just as our Lord allowed Himself to be beaten for our transgressions. Jesus is the Light, and He became the Light of the world (John 9:5) by obediently submitting to the Father.

Through the anointed ministry of the church, God shows us the way to the holy place. Inside, He leads us by the Light of the world, the Spirit of our Lord. The Spirit alone can guide us into the presence of God.

Directly across from the lampstand in the holy place stood the table of showbread. This again foreshadowed the Lord Jesus as the Bread of Life, whose body was broken for the world. The celebration of Holy Communion reminds us of His act of love. If we eat of the Bread, we will have eternal life.

> As the living Father sent Me, and I live because of the Father, so he who eats Me, he also will live because of Me. This is the bread which came down out of heaven; not as the fathers ate and died; he who eats this bread will live forever.
>
> —JOHN 6:57–58

The light from the lampstand illuminated the table of showbread in the holy place, just as the light of the Holy Spirit clarifies the bread of the Word. Whether we hear it in an anointed sermon during a worship service or in our personal devotions, only the Spirit-enlightened Word sustains us and renews our minds.

The third object in the holy place was the golden altar of incense, located directly before the veil that separated the holy place from the most holy place. Every morning and evening as the priests filled the lamps with oil, they burned incense upon this altar. For those of us who want to be true worshipers and to come into the Lord's presence, this step bears utmost importance.

Once again, the golden altar signifies God's requirement for purity and holiness because of His own nature.

> Your eyes are too pure to approve evil, And You can not look on wickedness with favor.
>
> —HABAKKUK 1:13

Before the incense could become a sweet-smelling aroma, the priests had to place it on a pure base. And so it is in our lives. The incense of pleasing worship to God emanates from a pure heart.

Indicative of the costliness of worshiping "in the beauty of holiness" (Psalm 96:9, KJV), priests carefully prepared incense for use in the tabernacle only. Three spices—stacte, onycha, and galbanum, combined in equal measure with frankincense and then tempered together by heating—comprised the special formula. After the priests evenly blended the ingredients into one, they crushed it into pieces suitable for burning before the Lord. Finally, only as fire consumed it did the incense release its heavenly scent. For our worship to be sweet to God, we must also undergo the same preparation.

According to A. P. Gibbs, four characteristics comprise a worshiper's heart. They seem to correlate to the four ingredients of the incense. The first heart element? Remembrance—focusing on the person and works of Jesus Christ. Then, gratitude, reverence, and finally, awe. These four parts undergo the same gentle tempering process as the Hebrews' incense. Too little or too much heat will destroy the elements rather than blend them together. The Holy Spirit, though, knows the exact temperature required to remove all the impurities in every believer.

After the Lord perfectly tempers our hearts, we're ready to begin the next step. Whereas the heating and blending may have been a bit unpleasant, this step can be downright painful.

But when we consider what the Lord endured to open the way for us into His presence, we have no right to expect total exemption from discomfort.

Priests beat the blended incense into small pieces before they burned it. In the Hebrew language, the word *daka* is translated as "beat; break in pieces."[4] The same applies to us. But we have already offered our bodies as living sacrifices in the outer court and our soulish intellect and emotions for His enlightening in the holy place. Now we should ask, In which part of our beings, then, does the crushing take place?

It still occurs in the holy place of the soul where our stubborn will resides. It needs to undergo an intense refining process. Our every desire must conform to God's purpose for us. We give up our "right" to have our own way. Once we voluntarily commit our lives to God, we relinquish complete control to Him. He becomes Boss. The results of the crushing of our old nature far outweigh any temporary pain. Our worship will rise as a pleasing aroma to the Father. As it is written, "The sacrifices of God are a broken spirit; A broken and a contrite heart, O God, You wilt not despise" (Psalm 51:17). He achieves this brokenness by divine fire in the same way the priests lit the incense.

So, first He consecrates our bodies, then our souls, and finally our spirits to Himself. The Lord Jesus underwent such an experience during His agony on the cross, as evidenced by His last words: "And Jesus, crying out with a loud voice, said, 'Father, into Your hands I commit My spirit.' Having said this, He breathed His last" (Luke 23:46).

When we, like Jesus, place our spirits into the hands of the Father, allowing Him to consume us by the fire of the Holy Spirit, we are prepared to enter into His presence. The perfumed smoke from the burning incense rose toward the four-colored ceiling of the ancient tabernacle. So our gaze, no longer looking straight ahead, fixes heavenward on the Lord in all His glory—perfect Man, suffering Savior, great High Priest, and King of kings.

The arrangement of the three objects in the holy place (golden lampstand, table of showbread, and golden altar of incense) form points of an imaginary triangle. This relates in a significant way to the love of God triangle we studied earlier (knowledge, covenant, and worship). From the illustration, we can see that each of the points "reflects" to the opposite side. By the light of the Holy Spirit (the lampstand), we grow in intimate knowledge of our Lord. As we eat the bread of the Word (the table of showbread) our covenant with Him deepens. Fervent worship (the altar of incense) releases a sweet fragrance toward heaven.

When we have come to know God intimately through Jesus Christ and have entered into a committed covenant with Him, when the fire of worship consumes us, then He will lead us through the veil into

the most holy place—the holy of holies.

Earlier we read that Jesus paved the way for us to pass through the veil and into the Father's presence. Now, because we have followed in the Lord's steps and have been prepared by the Spirit, we are ready to commune with God. Our great High Priest ushers us into the presence of the Almighty, much like the ancient high priest entered the most holy place to stand before the ark.

Under the old covenant, God allowed only the high priest to enter the most holy place, and even then only once a year to make atonement for the sins of the children of Israel. When he went in, he had to observe every single command and regulation. Any breach whatsoever

would cost the priest his life. The Lord directed him to bring incense
with him and set it in a specific place.

> He shall take a firepan full of coals of fire from upon the
> altar before the LORD and two handfuls of finely ground
> sweet incense, and bring it inside the veil. He shall put the
> incense on the fire before the LORD, that the cloud of incense
> may cover the mercy seat that is on the ark of the testimony,
> otherwise he will die.
>
> —LEVITICUS 16:12–13

We have already seen one implication of the incense and now we
find another. In Psalm 141 and in the book of the Revelation, incense
represents the prayers of God's people ascending to heaven.

> May my prayer be counted as incense before You; The lifting
> up of my hands as the evening offering.
>
> —PSALM 141:2

> When He had taken the book, the four living creatures and
> the twenty-four elders fell down before the Lamb, each one
> holding a harp and golden bowls full of incense, which are
> the prayers of the saints.
>
> —REVELATION 5:8

You may remember that the sole object in the most holy place was
the ark of the covenant with the mercy seat and cherubim on top of
it. Not even a ray of light detracted from the glory of the Lord in
that room. Two cherubim facing each other with outstretched wings
stood as silent witnesses of God's grandeur in heaven and on Earth.
The mercy seat reminds us that only God's infinite grace made a way
for us to come and commune with Him. We could never earn that
privilege based on our own merit.

> There I will meet with you; and from above the mercy seat,
> from between the two cherubim which are upon the ark of

the testimony, I will speak to you about all that I will give
you in commandment for the sons of Israel.

—Exodus 25:22

What did the priests store inside the chest-like ark? The stone
tablets with the Ten Commandments, a pot of manna, and the rod
of Aaron. These objects also bore witness to divine miracles and foreshadowed a new covenant in Jesus Christ. The stone tablets indicated
the inflexible law that God gave Moses and the rigid manner in which
He dealt with man in the Old Testament. Breaking His laws bore
fatal consequences, but Jesus fulfilled the Law. In the manna, we can
uncover another reference to Jesus as the Bread of Life from heaven.

What do we find in the rod of Aaron that speaks of our Lord? First
of all, the rod or stick verified the call of Aaron and his descendants to
the priesthood. God confirmed His choice of a spiritual leader when
He caused buds to form on a dead branch that belonged to Aaron.
This again prophesied of Jesus as the great High Priest who would
miraculously rise from the dead and as the One who would bring
new spiritual life to those who had been dead in sin. Even further,
the rod spoke of the restoration of the twelve tribes of Israel that will
occur during the Great Tribulation. Although the Israelites suffered
spiritual death when they rejected Jesus, they won't stay in that condition forever. New life will spring forth from that which seems dead.

The entire tabernacle illustrated the scope of God's dealings
with man through the ages and confirmed at least three important
facts: First, Jesus Christ is the same yesterday and today and forever
(Hebrews 13:8). Second, God has always desired and planned for man
to enjoy close fellowship with Him. And third, all that Satan stole
from Adam, Jesus bought back for both Jews and Gentiles, now and
forever. In Him, old and new merge to complete the restoration of our
relationship with the Father.

What a great God we serve! As true worshipers, we are to come
apart and be separate from the world, rather than letting it ensnare
us in its hustle and bustle. Then our lives will exemplify, even at
first glance, the transforming power of God's love. Evidence of our

assignment as "temples of the Holy Spirit" will be as obvious as the glory cloud over the ancient Hebrew tabernacle. Stay with us for the next chapter, and you'll find out more about how to make that a personal reality.

FIRE-SEEKER'S COMPANION

Questions for Group Interaction or Individual Reflection

1. Why study the details of the ancient Hebrew tabernacle? Why do you think more Christians don't take time to learn about it?

2. Where did the tabernacle stand in relation to the rest of the Israelites' wilderness camp? Who could pitch their tents near it and who had to remain at a distance? What does this arrangement say about worship today?

3. What enclosed the courtyard of the tabernacle and what does it mean? What four colors did they use for curtains at the gate and what do those colors symbolize? Going into the courtyard symbolizes what experience in the life of a believer? What does he learn to do there?

4. Describe the laver—what the Israelites used it for and what it means to you. Do the same for the brazen altar. Why was the laver before the altar? What covered the exterior of the tabernacle and why?

5. What three objects stood in the holy place and what do they symbolize?

6. Describe the most holy place. What does each have to do with you today?

7. How do you get into the most holy place, where you can truly worship the living God? Why do you want to be able to enter into that sanctuary?

Open Sharing: Feel free to discuss questions or anything related to the chapter that ministered to members of the group. Let the Holy Spirit lead you.

FIRE-STARTER'S PREPARATION

Spend time alone and together worshiping the Lord. Before and after, record your thoughts and feelings in a journal. Write down changes you notice in your life.

NOTES

Chapter Seven

PRAYER: THE HEARTBEAT OF WORSHIP

Prayer cannot be successfully separated from worship, for it prepares the soul for worship, expresses the spirit in worship, and interacts with God, which is worship. Worship without prayer is like daytime without light, a school without students, a choir without music, or an automobile without fuel...The praying saint cannot keep from worshipping, the prayerless saint cannot rise to worship.[1]

Prayer is the mold in which the character of our life is shaped.[2]

Prayer is the sap of the vineyard. When it flows, life will manifest itself, but when it ceases to flow, the leaves brown and fall off, the fruit withers on the vine, and the plant goes into the dormant stage. Prayer is therefore not elective but essential: no prayer—no life flow; no life flow—no fruit.[3]

Prayer must have priority. Prayer must be our bolt to lock up the night, our key to open the day.[4]

I GUESS WE'D BETTER get serious about prayer if we want a lifestyle of worship. Our goal is to practice the presence of God and maintain constant communion with Him. In the apostle Paul's letter to the church at Colossae, he wrote, "Devote yourselves to prayer, keeping alert in it with an attitude of thanksgiving" (Colossians 4:2). During the Lord's time of trial in the Garden of Gethsemane, He asked the disciples to pray. What did they do? They all fell asleep.

> So, you men could not keep watch with Me for one hour? Keep watching and praying that you may not enter into temptation; the spirit is willing, but the flesh is weak.
> —MATTHEW 26:40–41

No matter how strong the human spirit may be, as long as we're housed in earthly temples, we'll struggle to overcome the weaknesses of the flesh. But we can emerge victorious through watchful prayer. The disciples failed to pray, and look what happened to them. They scattered throughout the area. Peter even went so far as to deny the Lord, not once but three times.

True worshipers learn to be prayer warriors. We can't expect to "sleep," as Jesus called it, all week long and then run to church on Sunday to find the presence of God. Why wait? We can commune with Him every day.

Let me give you at least three very good reasons to pray. First and foremost: it brings honor to God. "Prayer is an act of worship, a paying homage" to our Father in heaven.[5]

Secondly, prayer develops humility by bringing us to the point of total dependence upon God. Continuing in prayer will lead us to the realization that without Him we can do nothing of lasting value. Paul summed up this thought in his letter to the Roman church when he wrote, "For I know that nothing good dwells in me, that is, in my flesh; for the willing is present in me, but the doing of the good is not" (Romans 7:18). Paul recognized his helplessness without God. Every true worshiper will discover this also as he learns to pray.

The third reason for prayer? So that we may receive what we need from God, for the Lord Himself, declared:

> Ask, and it will be given you; seek, and you will find; knock, and it will be opened to you. For everyone who asks receives, and he who seeks finds, and to him who knocks it will be opened.
>
> —MATTHEW 7:7–8

We don't mean to promote God as a kind of divine Santa Claus who grants us every single request. He gives us what we need, in line with His character. When we petition the Father in the name of Jesus, we pray for those same things He desires to give us, as outlined in His Word. We could say, in a sense, that we're "praying for God."

This may sound a bit unorthodox at first. But think about it. Prayer involves agreeing with God. We direct our prayers towards the accomplishment of His purposes in this world. He wants everyone to know Him. How often do we find our prayer time all but consumed with concerns for family, friends, and finances? Along with personal needs, we can pray that leaders, both among God's people and in the world, would be open to His Holy Spirit. The apostle Paul wrote about this to Timothy, his young helper.

> First of all, then, I urge that entreaties and prayers, petitions and thanksgivings, be made on behalf of all men, for kings and all who are in authority, so that we may lead a tranquil and quiet life in all godliness and dignity.
>
> —1 TIMOTHY 2:1–2

We can agree with God in prayer that He would show Himself strong on behalf of His people and that He alone would reign supreme in the kingdom of our hearts. One man named George Müller dedicated his life to helping orphaned children in England. Knowing that God had called him to that particular ministry, he depended entirely upon His support. George never asked for money. He relied on prayer and developed the following daily prayer vigil.

Each day, he read his Bible with expectation until he came upon something especially meaningful. He always read believing that God would give Him a specific word for the day. When He did, George wrote down what it meant to him. Then he meditated on the significance of the Scriptures and examined his thoughts, allowing the Holy Spirit to bring His ultimate purpose into focus. Finally, he spoke to someone about what he learned and how it related to him.

During his lifetime, George Müller became accustomed to starting each day in this way. If you haven't already discovered the benefits, you might consider developing similar habits. (We'll show you more about how to put these and other ideas into practice in the following section, "A Day-by-Day Lifestyle.")

Worshipful prayer goes beyond a mere morning routine. The Lord would like to guide our every step throughout the day, if we would listen to Him. Watching and praying enable us to hear His voice clearly. He has given every child of His the Holy Spirit to help in this area. During times of prayer we, like George Müller, receive guidance and direction that will keep us firmly in the center of God's will.

Another praying saint, Thomas Aquinas, noted that persistence in prayer consisted not of asking for many things but of desiring one thing: God Himself. This steadfastness brings about change in every parameter of our existence. Sincere prayer based on God's Word and led by His Spirit builds character. It establishes order in a once-fragmented life, because God is the author of order, not confusion.

Prayer exerts unbelievable demands on us. We might reach a stage where we'll have to decide to venture forth into uncharted territory. As we open our hearts and allow the Lord freedom, He will develop us in ways far beyond anything we, on our own, have ever attempted. True, worshipful prayer transcends the structure of ingrained behavior and rigid church traditions. In prayer, we can experience the holy and compassionate heart of the Lord.

C. H. Spurgeon once asked:

> Why is it that some people are often in a place of worship and yet they're not holy? It is because they neglect their [prayer] closets. They love the wheat, but they do not grind it; they would have the corn, but they will not go forth into the field to gather it; the fruit hangs on the tree, but they will not pluck it; and the water flows at their feet, but they'll not stoop to drink it.[6]

Achieving communion with the God of the universe is the essence and goal of worship. We can't hurry the process or neglect it. But realistically, how often in our daily routines do we find ourselves so caught up in the affairs of living that we squeeze in a few quick moments with the Lord? Those times when I'm too driven to pray, the "wheel falls off my race car," so to speak. Soon, I'm spinning toward a crash. Life ceases to be a joy.

We would do well to pursue our many interests only to the degree that we can stay relaxed. No more. When we pray and work, or pray and participate in sports, or pray and make love, all at a pleasant pace, life is great. Living like that prevents us from getting caught on the endless merry-go-round of obligations.

But committed Christians should roll up their shirtsleeves. We should work hard, you might be thinking. True, we should. In fact, Chuck Colson and Jack Eckerd wrote a great book on the subject entitled *Why America Doesn't Work.* Pushed to the extreme, though, we can easily fall into the "Martha syndrome." (See Luke 10:38–42.) She was doing important household tasks, but she missed the most crucial moments of all. Her industriousness kept her from resting at the feet of the Master to bask in His love.

A study of the meditative lifestyles of true worshipers reveals the ample time they set aside to live close to God and to listen for *rhema* (specific word) from Him. They have learned to obey the command to "be still, and know that I am God" (Psalm 46:10, KJV). John Wesley, a devout saint, described how he was able to achieve this: "Though I am always in haste, I am never in a hurry because I never undertake more work than I can go through with calmness of spirit."[7]

How do we continue in prayer, or, as the Scriptures read, "pray without ceasing" (1 Thessalonians 5:17)? First, by maintaining that open door we have received through the blood of Jesus. The lifestyle of worship is a life of forgiveness, even as the Lord forgives us— unconditionally. No unconfessed sin. No unforgiveness. We depend on Him to help us forgive every offense against us, whether real or imagined. In His Sermon on the Mount, Jesus told His followers, "But I say to you, love your enemies and pray for those who persecute you" (Matthew 5:44).

Motives in prayer are important to God. Selfish motives or prayers out of line with the Word fall short. A. W. Pink, in his lecture on the matter of scriptural prayer, wrote:

> The promises of God contain the matter of prayer and define the measure of it...Hence, the better we are acquainted with the Divine promises, and the more we are enabled to understand the goodness, grace, and mercy prepared and proposed in them, the better equipped we are for acceptable prayer.[8]

That may explain why some (not all) prayers go unanswered. Praying God's promises insures victory—eventually. Would you like to be a success as a prayer warrior? For all who answer "Yes," He prescribed a formula to Joshua as he was preparing to lead the Israelites into the Promised Land.

> This book of the law shall not depart from your mouth, but you shall meditate on it day and night, so that you may be careful to do according to all that is written in it; for then you will make your way prosperous, and then you will have success.
>
> —JOSHUA 1:8

God commands us, along with Joshua, to learn His Word and

speak it in prayer to receive His blessings. Then we'll be able to pray with the great expectation of His power being demonstrated in, through, and for us. Mouthing words or putting on the appearance of holiness with no inner transformation gets us nowhere. God knows the desires of our heart, and He wants us to hunger after His presence (Jeremiah 29:13).

A. W. Pink's mother taught him the following poem. How well these few simple lines express the need for sincerity.

I often say my prayers,
But do I ever pray?
And do the wishes of my heart
Go with the words I say?
I may as well kneel down
And worship gods of stone,
As offer to the living God
A prayer of words alone.[9]

Pink also wrote, "A life formed by prayer is a life opposed to illusion, self-deception, and hypocrisy...prayer is at war with falsehood."[10] These inward attitudes play a premier role in our ability to worship. Time after time in the Scriptures, we find our Lord confronting the pious appearances of religious leaders. In Matthew 23, He told them in no uncertain terms:

> Woe to you, scribes and Pharisees, hypocrites! For you clean the outside of the cup and of the dish, but inside they are full of robbery and self-indulgence. You blind Pharisee, first clean the inside of the cup and of the dish, so that the outside of it may become clean also...For you are like whitewashed tombs which on the outside appear beautiful, but inside they are full of dead men's bones and all uncleanness. So you, too, outwardly appear righteous to men, but inwardly you are full of hypocrisy and lawlessness.
>
> —Matthew 23:25–28

Hardly words of blessing. Jesus spoke for the Father, who wants hearts of loving obedience, not showy outward displays. His rebuke serves only to reemphasize the Lord's concern over our inner condition. We find in the book of Hosea another brief synopsis of God's priorities: "For I delight in loyalty rather than sacrifice, And in the knowledge of God rather than burnt offerings" (Hosea 6:6).

What does all this have to do with us today? We don't try to offer burnt offerings anymore. And though we may not consider ourselves as hypocritical as the Pharisees, we who have become "living temples of the Holy Spirit" still need regular cleansing. Just as Jesus drove out the unclean activities from the earthly temple in Jerusalem (designed as a house of prayer—Luke 19:46), so He purges us for prayer and through prayer. If we allow Him, He will accomplish this in each one of us.

When our "house" becomes such a cleansed and praying vessel, we can enter into the conscious presence of God to behold the glorious light of His countenance and commune with Him at the mercy seat. Such joy and peace as we experience there give us a tiny taste of all that awaits us in everlasting glory with Him.

FIRE-SEEKER'S COMPANION

Questions for Group Interaction or Individual Reflection

1. How do you feel about prayer? Does it have the importance in your life that the opening quotes emphasize?

2. What did the disciples do when Jesus asked them to pray during His hour of need? How long did He want them to pray? What happened to them when they failed to obey?

3. Why should you pray? Name as many reasons as you can.

4. What does "praying for God" mean? How does that differ from most people's prayers? How does it compare with yours?

5. Who was George Müller, and what made him stand out as a Christian? Name some other praying saints from history and some you know personally.

6. What are the keys to a meditative lifestyle?

7. When Jesus scolded the Pharisees, what did He say? How can you prevent that in your own life?

Open Sharing: Feel free to discuss questions or anything related to the chapter that ministered to members of the group. Let the Holy Spirit lead you.

Fire-Starter's Preparation

Spend time alone and together worshiping the Lord. Before and after, record your thoughts and feelings in a journal. Write down changes you notice in your life.

Notes

PART THREE

ALL-CONSUMING FIRE

Chapter Eight

A DAY-BY-DAY LIFESTYLE

FASCINATION. ADMIRATION. ADORATION. Veneration. Communion. These are all natural responses to a supernatural God! We demonstrate worship in a variety of ways. Authors Ronald Allen and Gordon Borror remind us, "We are not simply spirit beings. We are more than hearts or souls or 'inner beings.' We are persons possessing an intricate complex of physical and spiritual realities."[1]

Judson Cornwall learned for himself the truth of this, especially in the realm of individual responses to God. After speaking at a convention, he led the people into a wonderful time of praise and worship. The Lord urged him to take note of what the people were doing as they rejoiced in His presence. Some stood. Some danced. Others sang. Each worshiped in his own way. Without any human direction, the scene changed. Some, who had been standing, lay prostrate before the Lord, and some, who had danced, knelt and wept. All followed the leading of God in their hearts. As Judson watched this taking place, he heard the Lord say to him:

> The lesson I want you to learn is not to make people specialists in the expression of their worship. Allow for variety both corporately and individually. No one action can express all emotions, so allow for multiple actions in each person so that his or her worship can be complete.[2]

For easy reference we'll briefly summarize these avenues of expressing, in praise and worship, our love of God.

Voice

> I will bless the LORD at all times; His praise shall continually be in my mouth.
> —PSALM 34:1

> Be glad in the LORD and rejoice, you righteous ones; And shout for joy, all you who are upright in heart.
> —PSALM 32:11

> Praise the LORD in song, for He has done excellent things.
> —ISAIAH 12:5

> They shall speak of the glory of Your kingdom And talk of Your power.
> —PSALM 145:11

Silence

> But the LORD is in His holy temple. Let all the earth be silent before Him.
> —HABAKKUK 2:20

Hands

> So I will bless You as long as I live; I will lift up my hands in Your name.
>
> —PSALM 63:4

> O clap your hands, all peoples; Shout to God with the voice of joy.
>
> —PSALM 47:1

Body

> Come, let us worship and bow down; Let us kneel before the LORD our Maker. For He is our God.
>
> —PSALM 95:6–7

> With a leap he stood upright and began to walk; and he entered the temple with them, walking and leaping and praising God.
>
> —ACTS 3:8

> Let them praise His name with dancing.
>
> —PSALM 149:3

> Behold, bless the LORD, all servants of the LORD, Who serve by night in the house of the LORD!
>
> —PSALM 134:1

Instruments

> Praise Him with trumpet sound; Praise Him with harp and lyre. Praise Him with timbrel and dancing; Praise Him with stringed instruments and pipe. Praise Him with loud cymbals; Praise Him with resounding cymbals.
>
> —PSALM 150:3–5

No matter which of these responses we use to praise and worship the Lord, thankful hearts and sacrificial spirits mean the most to

Him. We don't worship to please men or show off to them but as a way of giving honor to God.

How about if we investigate the lifestyle of a true worshiper in today's world? We've cited many biblical examples of those who enjoyed a close relationship with God, but because of their remoteness, we may have a hard time envisioning ourselves in their places. In order to see the practical application of these principles, let's assume a privileged vantage point from which to "view" a day in the life of one such twenty-first-century worshiper. From there, what could we expect to observe?

Early in the morning, even long before the birds begin to greet the rising sun, Jake awakens. As he rubs the sleep from his eyes, he says in a hoarse voice, "Good morning, Lord. Thank You for one more day." During the next few moments as he throws off the covers, gets out of bed, and takes care of personal needs, he hums a gentle hymn of praise. Removing his Bible from its familiar spot on the nightstand (placed carefully there the previous evening before he fell asleep), he pads into the kitchen for a glass of chilled fruit juice. Then he's off to his favorite niche to spend precious moments with the Lord.

What began earlier as soft humming now grows into joyful song. Holding his Bible close to his heart and walking back and forth, he expresses how thankful he is for all God has done: the sacrifice and resurrection of Jesus, the cleansing power of His blood, forgiveness, new life, freedom from the bondage of sin, and above all else, eternal life with Him.

Over the years, Jake has learned the blessings of openly sharing his feelings with the Lord. As his time of praise and gratitude continues, we see him clap occasionally, lift his hands, and wipe away tears. Then something happens. God once again fulfills His promise to inhabit the praises of His people.

In mid-stride, Jake comes to a standstill and stops singing. We can hear him whisper again and again the name of Jesus. In gentle reverence, he lifts his hands, as if offering his very heart back to the Lord.

The sweet communion he feels radiates through the tranquil glow on his face.

Slowly he kneels in front of the easy chair and lets his Bible fall open to the Twenty-third Psalm. He reads the words in quiet affirmation of their truth. We hear him pray for his family (even Monarch), for his pastor and church leaders around the world, as well as for government leaders. His moving petitions flow forth—for their forgiveness and guidance—in each case according to the scriptural promises he knows by heart.

Last of all, we hear him pray that he would be a better husband. A more faithful servant. A better steward of God's gifts. He asks that he would be able to see everything from God's perspective rather than his own. Can you sense the fervor with which he pleads to be conformed to the image of Jesus?

As he starts turning the well-worn pages of his Bible, we hear one last petition for himself: "Lord, open my eyes so I can really see wonders out of Your law. Make Your Word alive to me and feed me my daily bread." Reaching into the drawer of the nearby end table, he brings forth his Bible study notebook and pen. He is prepared to receive God's directions for the day.

For the next hour or so he seems unaware of the passage of time. He reads, occasionally nodding his head and smiling, and then as a truth is revealed, he exclaims, "Thank You, Lord!" or "Hallelujah!" or "I praise You!" while he jots down a few lines in his notebook. Continuing in his daily Bible study, he moves to his desk, where, within easy reach are commentaries, a large concordance, and a Bible dictionary. Surrounded by the ponderous volumes, he glances at his watch and breathes a sigh of contentment. He still has half an hour to research the priceless truths earlier revealed.

Time slips by, and much to his dismay, he must set aside his favorite texts until later. All too soon, the moment arrives to get ready for the challenges of a day's work. Leaving the room, he sees his wife, Mary. She has just finished her time of personal devotions, and he greets her with "Good morning," a warm kiss, and an embrace.

With his arms still around her, he catches her enthusiasm as she says, "Hon, I've got good news. I think the Lord has given us an answer. If you hurry up and get ready for work, we can talk about it over breakfast." Humming softly to herself, she heads into the kitchen while he busies himself getting dressed.

A short time later, his nose leads him to the source of the wonderful aroma wafting through the house. He wanders into the kitchen, Bible and notebook in one hand and jacket tossed casually over his shoulder. "Mmm, homemade muffins—just what I wanted. How'd you know, sweetheart?"

She smiles and sets down a delicious breakfast before him and one at her own place. He takes her hand, they bow their heads, and he invites the Lord to bless the food.

Having finished his meal, he says, "That was great, hon. Sure am glad I married you." Then he pauses. "Let's hear what the Lord showed you this morning. You're pretty excited about it."

"Well, I think we're supposed to go ahead and accept the pastor's offer. I feel right about it. The Lord seemed to be saying that now is the time for us to step out in faith." Jumping up from her chair, she grabs the Bible, opens it, and points to a verse. "Here is our answer."

He chuckles aloud as his eyes slowly scan the words. Then he stands up and gives her a big hug. "That's great, hon. Wait 'til I show you what the Lord told me this morning, too." He grins as he picks up his notebook. Then he leads her over to their favorite love seat, waits for her to sit down, and puts his arm around her while opening the notebook on her lap. "Read this," he urges, indicating the passage.

She reads aloud, giving special emphasis to the words he had underlined:

> Brethren, I count not myself to have apprehended; but this one thing I do, forgetting those things which are behind, and reaching forth unto those things which are before, I press toward the mark for the prize of the high calling of God in Christ Jesus.

She sets the notebook down and looks up at him with tears in her eyes. "That's...the exact verse...He gave me!"

"I know. The Lord sure is faithful. So it's settled then. We'll call Pastor this afternoon and tell him we'll be honored to lead praise and worship. Let's pray now. It's almost time for me to go." They clasp hands and begin to pray for each other, calling upon God's protection and blessing. Completing their special time together, they walk hand in hand to the front door for one last hug before he leaves for work.

As he pulls into the space marked *Maintenance Supervisor* in the employee parking lot, Jake pauses a moment, listening to the last strains of the praise music coming softly through the radio. Climbing out of the car, he grabs the card with his Scripture memory verse for the day and heads to his office. A coworker awaiting their regular prayer group greets him with enthusiasm, "I really look forward to these few minutes we have before work. It sure makes a big difference."

Another worker wanders into the boiler room, and overhearing the conversation, adds, "Yeah, I don't know how we made it around here before."

Morning passes quickly. At noon, he picks up his Bible and the lunchbox that Mary packed for him and heads for his favorite dining spot out by the pond. It's so peaceful there with the ducks at play in the water. He smiles when he finds the love note tucked underneath his sandwich and breathes a prayer of thanks for such a great companion. When he's done eating, he reads some psalms and proverbs and concentrates on his memory verse until the end of the lunch hour.

The afternoon poses a few minor crises for him, most of which he handles with calm efficiency—a composure resulting from the assurance that Someone far greater than himself is in control. It wasn't always that way. Time was, when he rushed off to work late, agitated and anxious about what problems the day would bring. How well he knows that Jesus does, indeed, make a difference. His grace is always sufficient (2 Corinthians 12:9).

Afternoon rush-hour traffic on the way home, enough to make anyone lose his temper, is no longer the harrowing, white-knuckled experience it used to be. Instead, Jake offers a sacrifice of praise, singing familiar Scripture songs of victory. He looks forward to the fellowship he and his wife will have that evening with friends.

As he turns into their street, he hears the faint barking of a dog. At the driveway, an exuberant bundle of four-legged energy meets him. "Monarch!" he exclaims. "Are you glad to be back from the vet, old boy? Sure missed you this morning!" Monarch continues to bark and run in circles, bounding and leaping about as he trots beside his master into the house. "Say, I've got to call the pastor right away, tell him our decision."

Once inside, his sweetheart of twenty-five years greets him passionately and escorts him to his easy chair in the den. "Supper will be ready soon, hon, so just relax 'til then."

"Can you spare a moment to come sit with me while I make that call to Pastor? We're a team on this assignment, so you need to be here." His thoughtfulness elicits a grateful smile in response, and she perches on the arm of his chair. Nearby, Monarch heaves a sigh of contentment.

A short while after dinner, surrounded by their friends, they excitedly share how God had spoken to them both that morning. They tell how, for the past week, they had been seeking guidance for a major decision. They had asked, and true to His Word, the Lord had given wisdom liberally. Knowing the responsibility involved in leading and teaching worship, they needed the assurance that it was, in fact, God's will for them.

Once the friends have gone home and just the three of them—Jake, Mary, and Monarch—are alone again, they relax together. Husband and wife share the events of the day and enjoy one another's company. Opening a Bible one last time, they take turns reading aloud. Each offers insight into the passage and how they can apply it to their lives. Drawing to a close their time in the Word, they kneel down side by side to pray. As we leave our vantage point, we find Jake and Mary giving thanks for the blessing of their deepening walk with the Lord and looking forward to miracles yet to come.

What can we discover from this story? It may serve as one example of our goal: to live life as a worshiper. Worship varies from day to day and from person to person, of course, so we don't mean to suggest rigidly imitating Jake and Mary. But scriptural dynamics emerge from the story that we can use as a guide. All the major elements of worship we've discussed thus far come together in one practical illustration.

In review: God's invitation to worship extends to all people. He doesn't play favorites. The main character was not anyone unusual—just an ordinary workingman who loved the Lord. Most importantly, he kept God at the center of his whole life. When he got up early in the morning, his very first thoughts focused on the Lord.

Like the psalmist David, Jake had an obvious hunger to commune with God. He was more than willing to sacrifice a couple hours' sleep to have enough time with Him.

> O God, thou art my God; early will I seek thee: my soul thirsteth for thee, my flesh longeth for thee in a dry and thirsty land, where no water is.
> —PSALM 63:1, KJV

He freely expressed heart attitudes of humility and gratitude. Through songs of praise that led him into worship, he entered the sweet presence of the Holy Spirit. Although our worshiper enjoyed very close fellowship with the Lord, he still regarded Him with reverent awe.

He followed up his time of communion in song with Spirit-inspired prayer. Waiting patiently on the Lord, He prayed for the needs of others, for himself to be more like Jesus, and for God's will to be accomplished in the Earth. He read the Word with expectation, knowing God would provide guidance for his life. Next, he proceeded on with joy to a more in-depth study of the Bible in all its intricate beauty. Our worshiper had discovered there a source of unending fulfillment. He valued the Word so much that he carried it to work with him and even made out special cards with daily verses to memorize.

He shared deep love (nurtured by worship) with his cherished wife, and she followed his example in a commitment to early morning devotions. They each recognized that they were a gift to one another from the Father—their first love. Their lifestyle of worship gave birth to a desire to serve Him. As doors to ministry opened and God confirmed His will in that area, they stepped forward in faith. Their waiting showed not any hesitancy to serve but an acknowledgment of their total dependence upon the Lord for their service to be fruitful. In fact, this interdependent relationship was evident throughout the day.

At work, Jake asked God to be in control. For years, he had led a prayer group with his coworkers where his simple faith shined as a light to those around him. It resulted in calmness of spirit in spite of the circumstances that confronted him. Also, the joy of the Lord in his heart gave him a deep appreciation for nature, God's creation. In the evening, he and his wife got together with close Christian friends to fellowship and encourage one another. Their day closed like it began—with prayer and the Word, but this time together as a family.

> Evening, and morning, and at noon, will I pray, and cry aloud: and He shall hear my voice.
>
> —Psalm 55:17, kjv

> I will bless the Lord at all times; His praise shall continually be in my mouth.
>
> —Psalm 34:1

This is nonstop worship of our wonderful Lord! In any endeavor, practice makes perfect. As Judson Cornwall stated, "Worship is best learned by worshiping."[3] What begins with the seed of decision in our hearts and springs up to bud in the soil of everyday life will come to full bloom as we find our place in congregational worship. Just as the bloom comes after the bud, so, too, does worship in the assembly grow out of personal, daily worship. Allen and Borror expressed this thought beautifully:

> …all of life becomes a worship service. If Christians were devotedly practicing this lifestyle, a corporate service could not miss being a great blessing, for it would simply be a continuation of a worship service begun days (or weeks or months) before.[4]

FIRE-SEEKER'S COMPANION

Questions for Group Interaction or Individual Reflection

1. Do all people worship God the same? Why or why not? How do you feel about that?

2. List as many ways to worship God as you can. Which ones are you most comfortable with and why? Which new ways would you be willing to try?

3. Describe the early morning activities of our worshiper, Jake. Compare and contrast that with your own life. Do you need some improvement?

4. How did Jake apply his love of God to his workday? What can you do to worship God all day long?

5. Evening was a special time for Jake, too. Note some things he and his wife did that would help you in your walk with the Lord.

6. Individual worship during the week leads up to what event in the life of a believer? Why this natural progression?

7. What can you do, with God's help, to develop a lifestyle of worship? Are you willing to try? What results do you think you will see?

Open Sharing: Feel free to discuss questions or anything related to the chapter that ministered to members of the group. Let the Holy Spirit lead you.

Fire-Starter's Preparation

Spend time alone and together worshiping the Lord. Before and after, record your thoughts and feelings in a journal. Write down changes you notice in your life.

Notes

Chapter Nine

CELEBRATING GOD TOGETHER

*As a thoughtful gift is a celebration of a birthday, as a special
evening out is a celebration of an anniversary, as a warm eulogy
is a celebration of life, as a sexual embrace is a celebration of
a marriage—so a worship service is a celebration of God.[1]*

W E ALL VALUE those times when the family gathers for
special occasions. Festivities shared with others we love
lend a certain significance to life's major happenings
and serve to remind us that we belong to someone, that we're part
of a family. Behind every successful celebration lies much planning
and effort. The same holds true for the corporate celebration of God.
Our individual lifestyles of worship culminate in the weekly worship
service. According to Allen and Borror, "We must understand that
getting anything out of worship depends directly on our willingness
to put effort in to it!"[2]

This may mean allowing God to make major changes in personal attitudes, habits, and use of time. That, in itself, challenges us enough, but when we come together in fellowship with other believers, we face added difficulties. However great the challenge, it's well worth the effort. In the same way a gardener cultivates the earth before anyone can enjoy the beautiful aroma of a rose, the body of believers undergoes a kind of cultivation process. The flower of worship will come to full bloom and emanate a heavenly fragrance to the Father only after He has prepared the ground.

A lost world cannot help but be drawn to and affected by the true body of Christ when it worships in harmony. Like the early believers in the book of Acts, the church today would be better able to make an impact.

> And when they heard this, they lifted their voices to God with one accord and said, "O Lord, it is You who made the heaven and the earth and the sea, and all that is in them.… "And when they had prayed, the place where they had gathered together was shaken, and they were all filled with the Holy Spirit and began to speak the word of God with boldness. And the congregation of those who believed were of one heart and soul.
>
> —ACTS 4:24, 31–32

"Many go to church. Few go to worship," announced a church billboard in Nashville. How accurate! The Christian community practices its beliefs in many ways, but does a desire to worship form the basis for all our activity? In the meetings, there may be preaching, confession of sins and assurances of forgiveness, Scripture reading, communion, and baptism. The church sanctions marriages, participates in public prayer, and sings hymns. We may even be well known for musical ability, but what motive lies at the core of all these experiences?

Worship should be. Adoration of God should be at the center of every aspect of our lives. Activities, functions, and ceremonies take place in the name of Jesus, and yet His presence does not permeate them. If the worship we experience does not give us "courage in the night, joy in the dawn" and power for service, then it is only a mere facsimile of the real thing.[3] When we do all in His name to glorify Him, we approach genuine worship.

> Worship is the one religious activity that lends itself to such a delicate blending of different heritages, for worship is so Christ-centered and requires such a God-consciousness that participants must look away from themselves in order to worship.[4]

Unfortunately, more strife occurs because of differences of opinion about worship than perhaps any other area of faith. As Christians, we all agree on certain basic doctrinal truths, but we may have to remind ourselves of the need for individuality in worship. Within the bounds of Scripture, everyone needs the freedom to express his or her own heartfelt love of God. Our way is not the only way. Others may be just as sincere and growing equally as close to the Lord.

No matter what prior church experience we have, we struggle to achieve a scriptural balance in the three major dimensions of love. You may remember from our study of the love triangles in Chapter 2 that worship is the motivational factor. It spurs us on to acquire increased knowledge and to develop a stronger covenant with the Lord.

We noted the types of churches lacking the all-important component of worship. Either a man-made ritualistic formula or a pharisaical intellectualism characterizes the coldness of these assemblies. As we also mentioned earlier, ritual has some value if worship builds on that firm foundation. Congregational worship for the Old Testament Jews always began with ritual, proceeded on to worship, and finally continued to the high priest's oneness with God—one, two, three. Just as a man's bones give support and shape to his body, so, too, can meaningful ritual draw people together and lend solidity to worship.

In contrast to cold, dry churches, we learned that an overabundance of worship without an equal measure of the two remaining elements renders a body of believers just as unhealthy. For us to develop a positive, growing love relationship with God, all three components flow together in harmony. Indeed, maintaining this balance seems difficult enough in our personal walk. What happens in an assembly?

During congregational worship, our eyes tend to wander and focus on man rather than on God. If we find ourselves distracted by the way others worship, and if we allow personal prejudice to hinder us, we will be unable to sense God's glory. Those of us who grew up in traditional denominations may tend to shy away from people who lift their hands during prayer and worship. But why? It's only a symbol of releasing everything into God's more than capable hands. Besides, if the truth of the matter be known, much scriptural support exists for this practice, while there's no biblical precedent for the folding of hands.

> Lift up your hands in the sanctuary, and bless the LORD.
>
> —PSALM 134:2, KJV

> May my prayer be counted as incense before You; The lifting up of my hands as the evening offering.
>
> —PSALM 141:2

> Then Solomon stood before the altar of the LORD in the presence of all the assembly of Israel and spread out his hands toward heaven.
>
> —1 KINGS 8:22

> Therefore I want the men in everyplace to pray, lifting up holy hands, without wrath and dissension.
>
> —1 TIMOTHY 2:8

Setting aside preconceived notions and personal inhibitions is certainly not easy, but it is necessary. Other things also occur during communal worship that bring out our intolerance. However, the Scriptures exhort us throughout not to abandon the idea of getting together.

> Not forsaking our own assembling together, as is the habit of some, but encouraging one another; and all the more as you see the day drawing near.
>
> —HEBREWS 10:25

In every gathering of New Testament worshipers, we see, first of all, that they were committed followers of Jesus Christ. Christians today, as well as then, come together in the precious name of Jesus—in His honor and by His authority. Then we have a thrilling promise to believe in and proclaim: "For where two or three have gathered together in My name, I am there in their midst" (Matthew 18:20).

When we look to the early church for enlightenment about these gatherings, we see some situations well worth noting. Every assembly governed itself by the Word and was separated from the others because of distance only. In each locale, all believers came together as one group. Nowhere do we find reference to any such thing as denominations, only believers and unbelievers. In fact, the apostle Paul reprimanded those who did attempt to separate for one reason or another.

> Now I exhort you, brethren, by the name of our Lord Jesus Christ, that you all agree and that there be no divisions among you, but that you be made complete in the same mind and in the same judgment....Has Christ been divided? Paul was not crucified for you, was he? Or were you baptized in the name of Paul?
>
> —1 CORINTHIANS 1:10, 13

While adoration of God remains the primary purpose for congregational worship, mutual encouragement is another important reason for gathering together. Yet, this time of worship does not take place on a free-for-all basis. The Holy Spirit, if given freedom to move, will still maintain certain principles of order. God doesn't stir up confusion (1 Corinthians 14:33)! Paul's epistle to the Ephesian church tells us to rejoice together in the Spirit of God rather than to seek earthly bliss.

> Speaking to one another in psalms and hymns and spiritual songs, singing and making melody with your heart to the Lord.
>
> —EPHESIANS 5:19

What are the only restrictions he placed upon singing, dancing, shouting, weeping, and spiritual gifts? Do them to the glory of God and to build up His body, the church. In 1 Corinthians 14 we see a few guidelines concerning the use of spiritual gifts in a congregation.

> What is the outcome then, brethren? When you assemble, each one has a psalm, has a teaching, has a revelation, has a tongue, has an interpretation. Let all things be done for edification. If anyone speaks in a tongue, it should be by two or at the most three, and each in turn, and one must interpret; but if there is no interpreter, he must keep silent in the church; and let him speak to himself and to God. Let two or three prophets speak, and let the others pass judgment.
>
> —1 CORINTHIANS 14:26–29

In the book of 1 Timothy, Paul encouraged saints to read the Word as an essential part of group worship: "Until I come, give attention to the public reading of Scripture, to exhortation and teaching" (1 Timothy 4:13). Paul also urged that the various congregations share his letters. This kept the lines of communication open and promoted evenly balanced growth throughout the entire body of Christ (1 Thessalonians 5:27, Colossians 4:16).

Yes, all of these activities should take place during a worship service based on biblical principles. If we want to revitalize our love relationship with God, then we must seek to restore worship to its rightful position. Let's look at some scriptural examples of congregational assemblies where the glory and power of God came to dwell—even in the Old Testament before Jesus came in the flesh.

Shortly after David, as king of Israel, defeated the Philistine army from Geba to Gazer, he brought the ark of God to the city of Jerusalem. The whole nation of Israel turned out for this great event. Second Samuel 6 describes the entire account, but we'll concentrate on those verses pertaining to praise and worship.

> Now David again gathered all the chosen men of Israel, thirty thousand....Meanwhile, David and all the house of Israel were celebrating before the LORD with all kinds of instruments made of fir wood, and with lyres, harps, tambourines, castanets and cymbals...And so it was, that when the bearers of the ark of the LORD had gone six paces, he sacrificed an ox and a fatling. And David was dancing before the LORD with all his might, and David was wearing a linen ephod. So David and all the house of Israel were bringing up the ark of the LORD with shouting and the sound of the trumpet.... So they brought in the ark of the LORD and set it in its place inside the tent which David had pitched for it; and David offered burnt offerings and peace offerings before the LORD. When David had finished offering the burnt offering and the peace offering, he blessed the people in the name of the LORD of hosts.
>
> —2 SAMUEL 6:1, 5, 13–15, 17–18

Although there was order in everything that took place, freedom and joy flowed in their worship. In spite of the criticism King David's wife voiced for his lack of "propriety," he was committed to worshiping the Lord with all his heart.

Another example of superb congregational worship occurred when Solomon dedicated the newly completed temple. The priests had set the ark of the covenant in its position of reverence in the holy of holies, and the following took place:

When the priests came forth from the holy place (for all the priests who were present had sanctified themselves, without regard to divisions), and all the Levitical singers, Asaph, Heman, Jeduthun, and their sons and kinsmen, clothed in fine linen, with cymbals, harps, and lyres, standing east of the altar, and with them one hundred and twenty priests blowing trumpets in unison when the trumpeters and the singers were to make themselves heard with one voice…accompanied by trumpets and cymbals and instruments of music, and when they praised the LORD saying, "He indeed is good for His lovingkindness is everlasting," then the house, the house of the LORD, was filled with a cloud, so that the priests could not stand to minister because of the cloud, for the glory of the LORD filled the house of God.

—2 CHRONICLES 5:11–14

At this point, Solomon addressed all of the people and blessed them as they stood before the Lord. After a brief word to them, Solomon prayed and "kneeled down upon his knees before all the congregation of Israel, and spread forth his hands toward heaven" (2 Chronicles 6:13, KJV). David and the people had fulfilled God's requirements for coming into His presence. Note God's response and that of the people:

Now when Solomon had finished praying, fire came down from heaven and consumed the burnt offering and the sacrifices, and the glory of the LORD filled the house. The priests could not enter into the house of the LORD because the glory of the LORD filled the LORD's house. All the sons of Israel, seeing the fire come down and the glory of the LORD upon the house, bowed down on the pavement with their faces to the ground, and they worshiped and gave praise to the LORD, saying, "Truly He is good, truly His lovingkindness is everlasting."

—2 CHRONICLES 7:1–3

When the presence of Almighty God descended, the glory was so awesome that the priests could not even enter the temple. Imagine how humbling this was to all those present! They knew without a doubt that there was a God whose name was *Jehovah*. Their only response? Worship.

Let's look at one more Old Testament model of genuine communal worship, which took place during the time of the rebuilding of Jerusalem recounted in the book of Nehemiah.

> And all the people gathered as one man at the square which was in front of the Water Gate, and they asked Ezra the scribe to bring the book of the law of Moses which the LORD had given to Israel. Then Ezra the priest brought the law before the assembly of men, women and all who could listen with understanding....He read from it before the square which was in front of the Water Gate from early morning until midday...and all the people were attentive to the book of the law....Then Ezra blessed the LORD the great God. And all the people answered, "Amen, Amen!" while lifting up their hands; then they bowed low and worshiped the LORD with their faces to the ground. Also Jeshua....[and] the Levites explained the law to the people while the people remained in their place. They read from the book, from the law of God, translating to give the sense so that they understood the reading. Then Nehemiah, who was the governor, and Ezra the priest and scribe, and the Levites who taught the people said to all the people, "This day is holy to the LORD your God; do not mourn or weep." For all the people were weeping when they heard the words of the law.
>
> —NEHEMIAH 8:1–3, 6–9

John MacArthur, Jr. affirms a wonderful reality, saying:

> Worship is not an emotional exercise with God-words that induce certain feelings. Worship is a response built upon truth...If we are to worship in truth, and the Word of God is truth, we must worship out of an understanding of the Word of God.[5]

In the passage in Nehemiah, we can see the tremendous power of the Scriptures when read and explained to an assembly under the anointing of the Holy Spirit. It convicted them so much they cried. Oh, that we would have such power behind our teaching today!

We should never underestimate the importance of saints gathered together in worship to hear the preaching of the Word. *What do these examples have to do with us?* we might wonder. Since they occurred in the Old Testament before Jesus, do they apply to us today?

Yes. It's true, we do live under a new covenant with the Father now. No longer do we live bound to a regimen of Jewish law, but we enjoy grace by faith in Jesus. Love and dependence on Him gives us the ability to keep His commands and to worship Him fully. As we have stated, the manner in which God deals with us now differs from His treatment of the children of Israel prior to the birth, death, and resurrection of Jesus. Yet, neither His principles nor His desire for worship have changed.

> Jesus Christ is the same yesterday and today and forever.
> —HEBREWS 13:8

In his book *Real Worship,* Warren Wiersbe notes that someone asked him this same question. His reply, in part, was as follows:

> The Old Testament legal ceremonies were fulfilled in Christ, so we do not repeat them today. But I see no reason why we must make an artificial distinction between "Old Testament worship" and "New Testament worship" when we see no such distinction in Scripture.[6]

From the aforementioned patterns of worship, we can derive an all-important truth. In each case, worship took place in simple response to a manifestation or revelation of the glory of the Lord. Worship burst forth from the hearts of the people like a river overcoming a dam. How much more true should this be for us today who have the Spirit of God dwelling in our hearts?

Christ used the analogy of living water to describe the spiritual life that He came to make possible to all who believe.

> Everyone who drinks of this water shall thirst again; but whoever drinks of the water that I will give him shall never thirst; but the water that I will give him will become in him a well of water springing up to eternal life.
>
> —JOHN 4:13–14

This living water fills the believer at the new birth. It springs up within him in worship. It then flows out from him in service.

> If anyone is thirsty, let him come to Me and drink. He who believes in Me, as the Scripture said, "From his innermost being will flow rivers of living water."
>
> —JOHN 7:37–38

Long ago, Solomon made the observation that even though all the rivers ran into the sea, the sea never became any fuller nor the rivers emptier.

> All the rivers flow into the sea, Yet the sea is not full. To the place where the rivers flow, there they flow again.
>
> —ECCLESIASTES 1:7

For the spiritual river to flow freely through us, we have to first release it in worship to its ultimate Source. A. P. Gibbs rendered the following beautiful description of the source and destination of this powerful river within us: "The spiritual life which flows from God to us returns to Him in worship from us, and thus the divine cycle is complete."[7]

FIRE-SEEKER'S COMPANION

Questions for Group Interaction or Individual Reflection

1. What does a worship service have in common with birthday gifts/parties or an evening out with your mate on your anniversary? Does it have that excitement at your church? Why or why not, and what can you do?

2. What happened when believers got together in the book of Acts? Can that kind of impact happen again today? Who joins the celebration when Christians worship in unity?

3. What should be the goal of all church activities? Why does worship help bring people of many different backgrounds and personalities together? At the same time, what makes group worship a challenge?

4. Were there denominations in the early church? What separated believers? How were the different groups governed? Besides adoration of God, what should happen when believers worship together?

5. Describe the setting and reason for King David's grand worship service. What took place there? And King Solomon's service—what was it like, and why were they celebrating? How about the gathering under Ezra? Compare and contrast it with the other two.

6. What role does the Word of God play in congregational worship? Do Old Testament ceremonies apply to us? Why? What does each celebration we studied have in common with true worship today?

7. Compare a river with a lifestyle of worship. What does that mean to you? Would you describe yourself as exhibiting a trickle, a stream, or a fast-flowing river? What can you do about it?

Open Sharing: Feel free to discuss questions or anything related to the chapter that ministered to members of the group. Let the Holy Spirit lead you.

FIRE-STARTER'S PREPARATION

Spend time alone and together worshiping the Lord. Before and after, record your thoughts and feelings in a journal. Write down changes you notice in your life.

NOTES

Chapter Ten

OBSTACLES

GIANTS DWELL IN the land of worship. But, "God names the giants...presents His battle strategy, and leads on to victory. Worship is worth the warfare."[1] Such dangers have as their source, explained A. P. Gibbs, one or more of the following three things: "the devil, the infernal enemy; the world, the external enemy; and the flesh, the internal enemy."[2] Anything will try to climb on to the throne of our hearts, where God should reign.

In First Corinthians, Paul classified all mankind into three groups: natural, carnal, and spiritual man. The renowned twentieth-century Chinese preacher and teacher of the Word, Watchman Nee, wrote extensively on this subject. In his three-volume series *The Spiritual Man,* he defined these groups.

Natural man has been separated from God as result of Adam's sin and ensuing fall from grace. *Carnal* or soulish man has been redeemed from eternal death by belief in the blood of Jesus Christ. The Holy Spirit has come to live within him, but the flesh—his body and soul (mind, will, and emotions)—rules him. Only the *spiritual* man submits himself completely to the Holy Spirit. His human spirit, led by the Spirit of God, directs his body and soul.

Natural man cannot worship because he has no relationship with God. He is Creator to him but not Lord. Carnal or soulish man cannot experience true worship because his own humanity tosses him about. The spiritual man alone worships in the beauty of holiness because his spirit communes directly with the Spirit of God. He yields to the Holy Spirit's leading.

God has placed within every born-again believer the desire to worship. But the carnal man, because he does not walk in the Spirit, trips over obstacles and gets ensnared in pitfalls to worship. As Christians, we're *in* the world, but not *of* it. We have the power to say "No" to the selfish things of life and "Yes" to God and His commandments. To become true worshipers, we need to maintain that all-important balance in our love relationship with God and be willing to leave behind every obstacle and pitfall as vanquished foes. There is no other way.

Pride

Pride completely obstructs worship. It stands as our greatest stumbling block to a wonderful adventure.

> Pride is a subtle thing and often exists where it is least expected, for one can even be proud of his humility! Pride in one's own personal appearance leads that individual to give undue attention to himself or herself. Pride of gift leads to an ostentatious display of it and a secret craving for applause. Pride of position leads its owner to adopt a condescending air to his fellow believers. Pride of possessions shows itself in self-complacency and boasting. Pride of one's ecclesiastical position evidences itself in smugness and sanctimoniousness.[3]

Lucifer led worship in heaven. He walked closest to the throne of the Almighty until he became prideful and wanted to take God's place.

> You were the anointed cherub who covers [the throne], And I placed you there. You were on the holy mountain of God; You walked in the midst of the stones of fire. You were blameless in your ways From the day you were created Until unrighteousness was found in you.
>
> —EZEKIEL 28:14–15

This very fault of pride led to Lucifer's rebellion against God and to his ruin.

> How you have fallen from heaven, O star of the morning, son of the dawn! You have been cut down to the earth, You who have weakened the nations! But you said in your heart, "I will ascend to heaven; I will raise my throne above the stars of God, And I will sit on the mount of assembly in the recesses of the north. I will ascend above the heights of the clouds; I will make myself like the Most High."
>
> —ISAIAH 14:12–14

Closely associated with pride is the self-will Lucifer showed when he said, "I will do this" and "I will do that." We see another example of this obstacle in reference to two of the sons of Aaron, the high priest. These men knew the commandments of God regarding proper worship, yet they willfully disobeyed and paid a heavy price.

> Now Nadab and Abihu, the sons of Aaron, took their respective firepans, and after putting fire in them, placed incense on it and offered strange fire before the LORD, which He had not commanded them. And fire came out from the presence of the LORD and consumed them, and they died before the LORD.
>
> —LEVITICUS 10:1–2

Rebellious pride costs dearly. We have to come to Him on His terms, not ours.

Lack of Knowledge

You may remember from our study of the love triangle that a lack of scriptural knowledge not only keeps us from true worship, but we can be easily led astray, sometimes with harmful results. In Hosea, we see that a lack of knowledge serves as a poor excuse for disobedience. As the Scripture says, "My people are destroyed for lack of knowledge" (Hosea 4:6).

King David's disastrous first attempt to restore the ark of God to Jerusalem is a prime example. The ark represented the divine presence, the place where He communed with his people through the high priest. Scriptures plainly taught that only Aaron and his sons could touch the holy things of the tabernacle, while the sons of Kohath were to carry the ark on poles placed through rings on the top.

> When Aaron and his sons have finished covering the holy objects and all the furnishings of the sanctuary, when the camp is to set out, after that the sons of Kohath shall come to carry them, so they will not touch the holy objects and die. These are the things in the tent of meeting which the sons of Kohath are to carry.
>
> —NUMBERS 4:15

Since the ark had been missing from the house of Israel for many years, the people may have forgotten the prescribed method for transporting it. What actually took place? Second Samuel records the event.

> They placed the ark of God on a new cart that they might bring it....But when they came to the threshing floor of Nacon, Uzzah reached out toward the ark of God and took hold of it, for the oxen nearly upset it. And the anger of the Lord burned against Uzzah, and God struck him down there for his irreverence; and he died there by the ark of God.
>
> —2 SAMUEL 6:3, 6–7

Little did it matter that they tried to use a new cart to take the ark to Jerusalem or that they had good intentions in wanting to restore it there in the first place. Although God does look at our heart in preparation for worship, obedience to His previously stated commands is also important. We can be so thankful for the blood of Jesus, which cleanses us so that our sins might not keep us from the presence of a Holy God.

Independence

We have already used the expressions *dependence* and *interdependence*. These develop as our relationship with God deepens. An independent spirit will not long be tolerated in the presence of God. Wanting to be self-reliant and able to succeed on our own skills adds up to sin.

As teenagers, we all desired to be grown-up and out on our own in the world—independent from both God and family. During this period in life, many young Christians stray from the Father's embrace and attempt to "do their own thing." Also during this time they make many, sometimes tragic, mistakes as a result of a search for independence.

This is the exact opposite of abiding (making our dwelling) in God and His abiding in us. Jesus said unless we become like children, submissive and dependent, we miss out on His kingdom. Perhaps God tells us to raise our hands in worship as an outward indication of our inner dependency on Him—much like little ones who hold up their hands when they want to be picked up and held by a parent.

Critical Spirit

The habit of finding fault with everything and everyone devastates worship. It runs contrary to the attitudes and actions of Jesus, who seeks to deliver us from our sinful ways rather than simply condemn us. When we criticize rather than correct and encourage a brother, we condemn not only him but ourselves.

> Therefore you have no excuse, everyone of you who passes judgment, for in that which you judge another, you condemn yourself.
>
> —ROMANS 2:1

Many times we see faults in others that trouble us in ourselves. A critical spirit prevents us from becoming worshipers because it draws our gaze off of the perfection of God and onto the imperfections of mere men, especially *other* men. As long as we're pointing out another's weaknesses, we don't have time to allow God to cleanse us from our own sin. And holiness precedes entering His presence!

> Then you will call, and the Lord will answer; You will cry, and He will say, "Here I am." If you remove the yoke from your midst, the pointing of the finger.
>
> —ISAIAH 58:9

Laziness

Worship is active, not passive. It demands our all. Laziness should not even come up in the mindset of a true worshiper. Instead, the Scripture contains words like *seek, search, guard, fight, run, plant, sow, reap, build,* and *work...work...more work.*

> But prove yourselves doers of the word, and not merely hearers who delude themselves.
>
> —JAMES 1:22

> Poor is he who works with a negligent hand, But the hand of the diligent makes rich.
>
> —PROVERBS 10:4

In Matthew 25, Jesus told the story of a man taking a trip. Before leaving, he entrusted to three servants varying sums of money: five talents, two, and one, respectively. Two of the servants used what they were given wisely and multiplied it, while the third simply buried his share. Upon the master's return, he rewarded well the two productive servants, while he sent the third one away from his presence.

Obstacles

> But his master answered and said to him, "You wicked, lazy slave, you knew that I reap where I did not sow and gather where I scattered no seed....Therefore take away the talent from him, and give it to the one who has the ten talents. For to everyone who has, shall more be given, and he will have in abundance; but from the one who does not have, even what he does have shall be taken away. Throw out the worthless slave into the outer darkness; in that place there will be weeping and gnashing of teeth."
>
> —MATTHEW 25:26, 28–30

These examples, although given in terms of material wealth, speak also of spiritual treasure. We, as "joint-heirs with Christ" (Romans 8:17, KJV), have received much we can use for the glory of God. In order for the spiritual treasure to be multiplied and for us to be deemed good and faithful servants, we must share what the Lord has given to us. Like the two faithful servants who were diligent in their stewardship, looking expectantly for their master's return, we can do more than simply await the return of our Master and expect to be blessed.

A worshipful life requires much effort and self-sacrifice. The spiritually lazy person is not prepared to enter the presence of God. If we consider worship a duty rather than a passionate response to a loving God, slothfulness can result. When this happens, either individually or collectively, the fires of love grow cold.

Impatience

Failure to wait on God's go-ahead (taking things into our own hands) greatly hinders our relationship with Him. He directs us to rest in the Lord and wait patiently for Him (Psalm 37:7) and to be still and know that He is God (Psalm 46:10). If only we could learn to say with the psalmist, "My soul, wait in silence for God only, For my hope is from Him" (Psalm 62:5).

Impatience, in direct opposition to God's commands, may lead to even greater sins. Saul, the king of Israel, demonstrated the weakness of impatience while awaiting the return of Samuel, the prophet. The Lord had anointed Samuel as a priest, whose duty included leading the sacrificial worship before armies left for war. Saul overstepped his bounds and decided to perform the ceremony himself. This one act of disobedience had far-reaching consequences.

> Now he waited seven days, according to the appointed time set by Samuel, but Samuel did not come to Gilgal; and the people were scattering from him. So Saul said, "Bring to me the burnt offering and the peace offerings." And he offered the burnt offering. As soon as he finished offering the burnt offering, behold, Samuel came; and Saul went out to meet him and to greet him....Samuel said to Saul, "You have acted foolishly; you have not kept the commandment of the LORD your God, which He commanded you, for now the LORD would have established your kingdom over Israel forever. But now your kingdom shall not endure. The LORD has sought out for Himself a man after His own heart."
>
> —I SAMUEL 13:8–10, 13–14

Saul's failure to wait upon God's man proved disastrous, not only to his worship but to his future. Likewise for us. Jesus alone has earned the right to be our High Priest who leads us into the presence of God and on to fulfillment in our calling.

Legalism

Do you find yourself doing more and worshiping less? Unable to find time to sing and praise the Lord or to rest in His presence? The need for constant spiritual activity may be associated with the sin of pride. We might be seeking significance through our own works instead of the finished work of Christ. Responsible "Marthas" have their place, but not to the extent that busyness interferes with an ability to listen, worship, and grow in a love of God. Jesus' words to Mary and Martha give us a hint about performance-oriented legalism.

> She had a sister called Mary, who was seated at the Lord's feet listening to His word, But Martha was distracted with all her preparations; and she came up to Him, and said, "Lord, do You not care that my sister has left me to do all the serving alone? Then tell her to help me." But the Lord answered and said to her, "Martha, Martha, you are worried and bothered about so many things; but only one thing is necessary, for Mary has chosen the good part, which shall not be taken away from her."
>
> —LUKE 10:39–42

Emotionalism

Human emotions can hinder the development of a worshiper's heart if they are allowed to rule, unchecked by wisdom. Different emotions affect people in various ways. Unfortunately, the majority have either long or short-range negative consequences. Most of us have had at least a passing acquaintance with anger, anxiety, or depression at one time or another.

During the rebuilding of the wall around Jerusalem, the people reacted emotionally to the enemy's efforts to hinder their project. They became discouraged and unable to work.

> Thus in Judah it was said, "The strength of the burden bearers is failing, Yet there is much rubbish; And we ourselves are unable To rebuild the wall."
>
> —NEHEMIAH 4:10

Elitism

This phenomenon in the church departs from the truth of the Word. It has wrought havoc in the body of Christ. Wherever the truth— all believers as priests unto the Lord—has been exchanged for the exclusivity of the clergy, it has very nearly destroyed Christians' ability to worship. E. H. Broadbent's *Pilgrim Church* points out how, by forming a special caste called "clergy" who bear the full responsibility of going before God on behalf of believers, some mainline denominations have departed from the spirit of the New Testament church. Through His victory on the cross, Jesus established the priesthood of all believers. Any Christian may go boldly before Him to receive grace. This became evident when the veil between the holy and the most holy places was torn in two at the moment of His death.

> You also, as living stones, are being built up as a spiritual house for a holy priesthood, to offer up spiritual sacrifices acceptable to God through Jesus Christ.…But you are a chosen race, a royal priesthood, a holy nation, a people for God's own possession, so that you may proclaim the excellencies of Him who has called you out of darkness into His marvelous light.
>
> —1 PETER 2:5, 9

Traditionalism

Many times, worship is compromised by theology instead of theology being permeated with worship. Endless questions about nonessentials detract from worship and stifle faith. Formalism, the outward observance of forms, rules, and methods carried to extremes, quenches the Holy Spirit. Do our traditions enhance, rather than hinder, worship? That's the crucial question. Judson Cornwall summed up this idea when he said:

> To insist upon doing only what comes naturally is to limit ourselves to the peer pressure and cultural restraints others have place upon us, and this means that we will never rise to a level higher than that which others have chosen for us to attain.[4]

> Now the Lord is the Spirit, and where the Spirit of the Lord is, there is liberty.
>
> —2 CORINTHIANS 3:17

Unforgiveness

Harboring unforgiveness against anyone, whether for real or imagined wrongs, hinders worship. In order to enter God's presence, we must be forgiven and cleansed from all sin.

> Behold, the LORD's hand is not so short That it cannot save; Nor is His ear so dull That it cannot hear. But your iniquities have made a separation between you and your God, And your sins have hidden His face from you so that He does not hear.
>
> —ISAIAH 59:1–2

God won't forgive us if we refuse to forgive others for their offenses. Our Lord makes this clear in the Sermon on the Mount.

> And forgive us our debts, as we also have forgiven our debtors....For if you forgive others for their transgressions, your heavenly Father will also forgive you. But if you do not forgive others, then your Father will not forgive your transgressions.
>
> —MATTHEW 6:12, 14–15

Unforgiveness devastates communion with God. Whether in the Old Testament or in the New, the Word states repeatedly that the only way to come into His presence is with a heart free from sin. Until we choose to forgive everyone of every wrong against us, worship will be impossible.

Worldly Influence

The fires of worship will never burn in a heart tainted with an affection for worldliness. The reason for this is simple: no man can serve two masters. He will love one and hate the other. Once we have been born again by the Spirit of the Lord, in essence, we no longer belong to this world. We become strangers passing through a foreign land en route to an eternal, heavenly kingdom. When we know this fact, we'll find it easier to say "No" to the world's temporary attractions. Yet, its influence can creep into our lives insidiously if we close our eyes to its dangers. For this reason Jesus prayed:

> I do not ask You to take them out of the world, but to keep them from the evil one. They are not of the world, even as I am not of the world.
>
> —JOHN 17:15–16

> Do not love the world nor the things in the world. If anyone loves the world, the love of the Father is not in him. For all that is in the world, the lust of the flesh and the lust of the eyes and the boastful pride of life, is not from the Father, but is from the world.
>
> —1 JOHN 2:15–16

Because of the strong magnetic pull of our flesh, the Bible advises us to not even fellowship with those involved in lusty pursuits. Although we're called to love and minister to them so they might also know Christ, we must remain free from their habits. That's a hard balancing act. Concerning this dangerous influence, we see one more admonition from the apostle Paul.

> Do not be bound together with unbelievers; for what partnership have righteousness and lawlessness, or what fellowship has light with darkness?...."Therefore, come out from their midst and be separate," says the Lord.
>
> —2 CORINTHIANS 6:14, 17

This separation involves more than just an outward physical separation. How about the realm of thought life? We can sit in church and, from all outward appearances, be gloriously worshiping the Lord. Meanwhile our mind stays preoccupied with the cares of life. But we can't fantasize about an affair or think about the latest sale at the mall and worship. God deserves our undivided attention.

Consider Lot's wife and the influence that the perverse city of Sodom held over her. When an angel commanded the family to leave

Sodom before the Lord would destroy it by fire, she looked back. She was destroyed along with the rest of the city.

Though attractively camouflaged, Satan uses the things of the world for one ultimate goal—to cause us to spend eternity separated from God. If we forego fellowship with darkness, we'll be able to have sweet communion with Him who is Light.

FIRE-SEEKER'S COMPANION

Questions for Group Interaction or Individual Reflection

1. The apostle Paul and Watchman Nee classified people into three spiritual categories that line up with the Word. What are they? Describe the differences and how they affect worship. How would you rate yourself?

2. Give some examples of pride. What does pride have to do with Satan (formerly Lucifer) and worship? With you?

3. How did Nadab and Abihu sin, and what were the consequences? What happened to Uzzah and why? How do these stories apply to you?

4. How does independence affect worship? A critical spirit? Laziness? Why did Saul's impatience get him in trouble? Do these same ones hinder you?

5. How did legalism make Martha behave? Contrast her with Mary. What hindered the rebuilding of the wall in Jerusalem? Does the same happen to you as you try to do something "as unto the Lord"?

6. Elitism—give an example of it and explain its negative influence on freedom of worship. How about traditionalism?

7. What is the danger of unforgiveness in relation to worship? Can you pray for those "who spitefully use you"? Worldliness keeps us from worshiping God. Why? What happened to Lot's wife?

Open Sharing: Feel free to discuss questions or anything related to the chapter that ministered to members of the group. Let the Holy Spirit lead you.

Fire-Starter's Preparation

Spend time alone and together worshiping the Lord. Before and after, record your thoughts and feelings in a journal. Write down changes you notice in your life.

Notes

Chapter Eleven

PITFALLS

MORE DANGERS LURK on the path to worship. Most have inherent positive value, but they can easily turn into idols—inappropriate objects of worship. When anything receives higher priority than God, we might as well fall into a dark pit. We lose sight of our first love! The foremost commandments reflect His feelings about this issue.

> Hear, O Israel! The LORD is our God, the LORD is one! You shall love the LORD your God with all your heart and with all your soul and with all your might.
>
> —DEUTERONOMY 6:4–5

> You shall have no other gods before Me.
>
> —EXODUS 20:3

We may need to take a close look at priorities and bring them back into perspective. To protect ourselves against idolatry, it helps to recognize who hides behind the scenes trying to steal what rightfully belongs only to God. Satan wants to replace God as the lord of our heart and make us bow in obeisance to him. The devil even tempted Jesus at the beginning of His earthly ministry.

> Again, the devil took Him to a very high mountain, and showed Him all the kingdoms of the world and their glory; and he said to Him, "All these things will I give You, if You fall down and worship me."
>
> —MATTHEW 4:8–9

We have observed from reading of Lucifer's fall from heaven that pride caused his demise. In this conversation with Jesus, he was up to his old tactics. Did he try to get the Lord to worship him? Yes. And we can believe he tries the same with us today.

Most of us think of idols as something we can touch with our hands, such as the false gods or statues of pagan religions. Idolatry is much more common than that. Pagans do bow down to idols, yet more often, modern idolatry takes on a far subtler form in the heart rather than the hands. Satan's attempts to steal our worship of the one true God are extremely deceptive and rarely take the form of a direct frontal attack. Instead, he prefers to sneak in the side door, catching us unaware. To help expose his strategy, we will look at some of our most vulnerable areas.

Self

As far as worship goes, we're our own worst enemy. Our society, especially in America, promotes a philosophy of immediate self-gratification as one of the highest standards of living. Magazines with titles that encourage exaltation of self sell on nearly every magazine rack.

Self-centeredness runs rampant today. Everywhere people in love with themselves boast about their abilities and accomplishments and give no credit to God. Instead, we hear of self-improvement courses, self-esteem, self-will—self, self, self! I once heard the saying, "The trouble with a self-made man is he worships his creator." If we ever want to become worshipers of the living God, we'll have to pull this demonic philosophy out of our lives by the roots. It's called *humanism*. In 1933, the Humanist Manifesto suggested that the universe was self-existent, not created. It declared war against any belief in the supernatural and the unique religious emotions and attitudes that go hand in hand with that belief. The humanists denied the spiritual foundation upon which our forefathers built this nation. Man alone was responsible for the realization of his dreams—the master of his fate. Contained within man himself was the power for all great achievement, they said. They even felt bold enough to state that God was dead. How contrary to the Scriptures, which say, "It is better to trust in the LORD than to put confidence in man" (Psalm 118:8, KJV).

We can never be humble enough before God to worship Him if our own personal desires rule. Notice again the tactic Satan uses. In his temptation of Eve, he attacked her in the area of her self-centered wants.

> When the woman saw that the tree was good for food, and that it was a delight to the eyes, and that the tree was desirable to make one wise, she took from its fruit and ate; and she gave also to her husband with her, and he ate.
>
> —GENESIS 3:6

Unless we want to succumb to the same subtle temptations, we must deny ourselves, take up our crosses, and follow the Lord with all our hearts. That may be easier said than done, but not if we consider the extent to which Jesus denied Himself for us. With every fiber of His being crying for life, He submitted to His Father's will and died so that we might live.

Family

The Bible says a great deal about the family relationship. Marriage symbolizes the union between Jesus and His bride, the church. Thus, He expects husbands to love their wives the way He loves the church and wives to revere their husbands the way the church reverences Him. In turn, as parents they train their children according to scriptural principles of love and discipline.

Any time a family fails to follow God's divine order (as when the husband allows the wife to "rule the roost" or when children's demands override God's commands, which is idolatry), confusion and strife ensue. Eli, a priest of Israel, lost the right to lead worship because he had allowed his sons to control him and rebel against God. They did whatever they pleased. The Lord told the prophet Samuel in a vision:

> "In that day I will carry out against Eli all that I have spoken concerning his house, from beginning to end. For I have told him that I am about to judge his house forever for the iniquity which he knew, because his sons brought a curse on themselves and he did not rebuke them. Therefore I have sworn to the house of Eli that the iniquity of Eli's house shall not be atoned for by sacrifice or offering forever."
>
> —1 SAMUEL 3:12–14

Possessions

Things we own—homes, cars, clothes, or conveniences—may become idols in a hurry. The key to preventing this? Realize we're only temporary stewards of any possessions and not the true owners. Our Father in heaven owns everything. He just lets us use some of it for a while. In Matthew 6:19–21, Jesus taught the value of maintaining the proper priority regarding possessions:

> Do not store up for yourselves treasures on earth, where moth and rust destroy, and where thieves break in and steal. But store up for yourselves treasures in heaven, where neither

moth nor rust destroys, and where thieves do not break in or steal; for where your treasure is, there your heart will be also.

Believers in the book of Acts realized this fact and conducted their lives accordingly. They shared with one another, not out of coercion as in communism but out of love.

> And the congregation of those who believed were of one heart and soul; and not one of them claimed that anything belonging to him was his own, but all things were common property to them....For there was not a needy person among them, for all who were owners of land or houses would sell them and bring the proceeds of the sales.
>
> —ACTS 4:32, 34

During those days, the greatest revival of worship in history took place. Signs and wonders were prevalent and everyone spoke the Word of God with boldness. It must have been a glorious time when the Holy Spirit moved so mightily among men!

Power

"Power corrupts, and absolute power corrupts absolutely," stated a wise man. This expression holds true for today's church as much as for those involved in the world's system. Believers are just parts of the body of Christ. He alone is the all-powerful Head. Even in the early church, some people hungered for control over others. Diotrephes sought a prominent position, as John pointed out: "I wrote something to the church; but Diotrephes, who loves to be first among them, does not accept what we say"(3 John 9).

Compare this to Jesus' remarks to the ten disciples after the mother of James and John requested the promotion of her sons to the top spot.

> You know that the rulers of the Gentiles lord it over them, and their great men exercise authority over them. It is not this way among you, but whoever wishes to become great

among you shall be your servant, and whoever wishes to be
first among you shall be your slave; just as the Son of Man
did not come to be served, but to serve, and to give His life
a ransom for many.

—MATTHEW 20:25–28

We have to continually examine and reexamine our motives to
insure that we desire to serve rather than be in a position of power.
God alone has the title of "Boss." We, like Paul, are His bondservants,
slaves by choice, if we want to be worshipers after His own heart.

Money

Money—the big scoreboard—is often worshiped in today's society.
People study the stock market with zeal but can't find a moment to
study the Word of Life. How many of us have looked to Wall Street
for security rather than to Jesus Christ? Money itself doesn't cause
problems, but the love of it does (1 Timothy 6:10).

Think of the tragic story of Ananias and Sapphira in the book
of Acts. During the time when the power of the Holy Spirit was
so mighty, people willingly sold their land and possessions in order
to give the money to the Lord's work. No one among them lacked
anything because of their obedience. Ananias and Sapphira were
obedient in selling their property, but they stumbled when the time
came to part with the money.

But Peter said, "Ananias, why has Satan filled your heart to
lie to the Holy Spirit and to keep back some of the price of
the land?…Why is it that you have conceived this deed in
your heart? You have not lied to men but to God." And as he
heard these words, Ananias fell down and breathed his last.

—ACTS 5:3–5

Sapphira's love of money caused her to follow in the steps of her
husband and suffer the same fatal consequence. Money as an idol
leads us all far from God. That doesn't have to happen. We can steer
clear of the danger associated with the love of money if we devote a

good part of our treasure to the God we worship. So spread the good news!

Occupation

Before we have experienced the joy of true worship, some of us find the business world much more invigorating. America encourages this. Professional success becomes a god of this world. People often feel condemned if they don't spend fifteen hours a day at the office and several more at home with paperwork. "God's Word recognizes the necessity for the Christian to be in business, but warns against business being in the Christian."[1]

The apostle Paul, a tentmaker by trade, used his job as a means of helping to support his ministry (Acts 18:3). Paul did not order his ministry around his job, and neither should we. Whether in full-time Christian service or not, we can still be good stewards who see an occupation as a platform to enhance God's business—the preaching of the gospel far and near.

Recreation

God has planned for us to enjoy the fruit of our labor. But when the enjoyment of this fruit becomes the sole purpose for laboring, idolatry, like a weed, has taken root. He is not a merciless taskmaster who requires constant work. However, recreation may compete for quality time with Him. When athletics (in itself inherently beneficial) prevents us from reading the Bible or from praying and worshiping God, we'd better regroup.

How much time and money do Americans spend in search of that elusive quality, pleasure? So much recreation offered by the world today does not align with Scripture, and it concerns me. I'm apprehensive about the effects it will have on my children and grandchildren because I know that even the best counterfeit is but a poor substitute for time with the Lord. Our choices can help us glorify God and still allow us to worship.

Paul, in his illustrations of the Christian life, made references to a runner in a race as well as a skilled boxer. He gave us the key to balance.

> For bodily discipline is only of little profit, but godliness is profitable for all things, since it holds promise for the present life and also for the life to come.
>
> —1 TIMOTHY 4:8

Recreation and good physical health can enhance our ability to worship. But replace it? Never.

Science

In today's world of expanding technology, science has become an idol—the one used most often to refute the truth of the Bible. When man's learning divorces itself from the knowledge of God, it usually opposes divine revelation found in the Scriptures. If we choose to place our faith in science above the truth of God's Word, idolatry results.

Have you heard about the conflict taking place in our nation's schools? It concerns teaching the theory of evolution versus the biblical account of creation. Evolution often gets better press; creationism is portrayed as a myth. Much of this debate rages around the seeming discrepancy between the age of the Earth and the length of man's existence on the planet. Yet, a closer look reveals the total awesomeness of our God and declares the absolute truth of His Word. Let's pursue this point a bit further in support of our glorious Lord.

As we first open our Bibles, we see in Genesis 1:1 that, "In the beginning God created the heavens and the earth." The ultimate beginning of creation! Prior to this, in the dateless past, God alone existed. When He created heaven and Earth, He included all the stars, the sun and moon, the Earth, and all the heavenly host: angels, cherubim, seraphim, and even that anointed cherub himself, Lucifer.

In the fourteenth chapter of Isaiah, and in the twenty-eighth chapter of Ezekiel, we read about the fall of Lucifer and learned that he was cast from heaven into the Earth.

> How you have fallen from heaven, O star of the morning,
> son of the dawn! You have been cut down to the earth.
>
> —ISAIAH 14:12

The Bible gives no record of exactly when this event took place. But we do know in Genesis 3 that Satan, disguised as a serpent, tempted Eve in the Garden of Eden. That means Lucifer had already lost his anointed position in heaven by that time.

A careful study of Scripture points to Lucifer's fall having occurred some time after the original creation in Genesis 1:1 and before the condition of the Earth as found in Genesis 1:2: "The earth was formless and void, and darkness was over the surface of the deep, and the Spirit of God was moving over the surface of the waters." How many years—perhaps millions—took place between these verses? And what occurred, we don't know.

Centuries after Adam and Eve, the prophet Jeremiah saw a vision of the Earth in the same condition that Genesis 1:2 describes. He recorded that vision and the causes that led up to a cataclysmic annihilation of life on the entire planet.

> I looked on the earth, and behold, it was formless and void;
> And to the heavens, and they had no light. I looked on the
> mountains, and behold, they were quaking, And all the hills
> moved to and fro. I looked and, behold, there was no man,
> and all the birds of the heavens had fled. I looked, and behold,
> the fruitful land was a wilderness, And all its cities were
> pulled down Before the LORD, before His fierce anger. For
> thus says the LORD, "The whole land shall be a desolation, yet
> I will not execute a complete destruction. For this the earth
> shall mourn And the heavens above be dark, Because I have
> spoken, I have purposed, And I will not change My mind,
> nor will I turn from it."
>
> —JEREMIAH 4:23–28

This desolation resulted from the Lord's fierce anger, but why was He angry? At some point during the vast time span between the original creation and the destruction, God threw Lucifer down to Earth, along with one third of all the angels. Lucifer had so perverted God's creation that He had to destroy it. Consider the description of the Earth as found in Genesis 1:2 and the one in Jeremiah's prophetic vision. They're nearly identical.

True to His Word, God did not make a full end of the Earth, but began again, as Genesis 1:3 indicates. Maybe what science calls the big bang theory refers to the moment God, the Creator, said, "Let there be light."

There is one final point of interest we can't ignore. After God created Adam and Eve, He gave them a specific command to "be fruitful, and multiply, and replenish the earth" (Genesis 1:28, KJV). How could they replenish the Earth unless it had once before been filled? We need not be deceived by the lies and tricks of the devil. He will go to any lengths to cause us to doubt the authenticity of God's Word, to subvert His authority, and ultimately, to destroy our worship of Him.

A. W. Tozer had a straightforward view of lofty matters.

> Science of course deals with the relation of things and their effect upon each other. But the plain people, the people who would rather believe than to know, and who would rather worship than to discover-they have a simpler and more beautiful view of the world.[2]

Occult

Millions of Americans saw a movie that came out in the early seventies called *The Exorcist.* It focused on a case of demon possession. However representative of Satan's work as the movie may have been, the devil usually poses in much more subtle and attractive ways. An article about modern-day witches that presented a disguised view appeared in *Insight: The Washington Times.*[3]

The article put forth some very disturbing misconceptions that tried to separate the occult practice of witchcraft from Satan. It was effective. Check out the following quotes from letters received in response to the article.

> Avoiding the false Hollywood stereotypes and correctly disassociating both witches and their religion from satanism, the article presented a view of their religion that is believable...

> Witchcraft is flourishing because of its positive benefits to its participants and the entire planet. Most rituals have some focus on healing our ravaged Mother Earth. Women especially are drawn to it because of the emphasis on a female divinity which has been denied us in all Western religions. I find it appalling that satanism is mentioned in the glossary of witchcraft terms. Satan has nothing to do with witchcraft, wicca or paganism. None of these groups even believe in the devil's existence. Most feel that Satan is a figment of the medieval church's collective imagination used to coerce people into becoming tithe-giving churchgoers.

We should make no mistake about these things. Behind all forms of the occult, whether under the guise of religion or not, lies the devil himself. The Word of God is quite clear about whom we worship and equally clear as to what occultish practices we should avoid.

> There shall not be found among you anyone who makes his son or his daughter pass through the fire, one who uses divination, one who practices witchcraft, or one who interprets omens, or a sorcerer, or one who casts a spell, or a medium, or a spiritist, or one who calls up the dead. For whoever does these things is detestable to the LORD; and because of these detestable things the LORD your God will drive them out before you.
>
> —DEUTERONOMY 18:10–12

This passage covers many activities that may go unrecognized and may be accepted as "harmless." Even something as seemingly innocent as reading the daily horoscope is risky business. In addition to astrology, the Bible includes warnings against palm reading, fortune telling, Ouija boards, and séances (attempting to speak to the dead).

The father of lies himself orchestrates such practices behind the scenes, and the Lord forbids all of it—including of course, blatant Satan worship. Sin of this nature affronts the omnipotence and guidance of God. The Old Testament punishment for these practices was severe: "He who sacrifices to any god, other than to the LORD alone, shall be utterly destroyed" (Exodus 22:20).

Although we no longer live under the Law, God's principles remain the same. He has not lowered His standards just because we now live under the dispensation of grace. If we want to become worshipers of the living God, we can't leave open doors through which Satan may gain an entrance. An idol doesn't become an idol overnight. It takes time. What may have seemed an innocent activity or a fun game at first leads to bondage. The Holy Spirit of truth will alert us to every dangerous practice if we listen. One author gives a few good guidelines:

> ...one of the obvious contrasts between response to the demonic and response to the Divine is that the demonic prefers a mindlessness or trance, but God always demands an active mind and will. Relationship with God in worship is for the entire person—spirit, soul and body—and we are invited to be willing and active participants in that experience.[4]

Questions for Group Interaction or Individual Reflection

1. What is the foremost commandment? Why? Is God on a super ego-trip? Explain idolatry. Does it happen in America? Who is behind it and why?

2. Self interferes with worship. Why? Define *humanism* and explain its dangers. How can one's family become a pitfall to worship? What happened to Eli?

3. How should we regard possessions? What did believers do in the book of Acts and why? How can a love of power or position inhibit worship? What did Jesus tell a status-conscious mother?

4. Is money a sin? What happened to Ananias and Sapphira, and why? Can something as necessary as occupation get in the way of communion with God? How can we avoid that? Is recreation evil?

5. Science hinders worship for many people. Why? What can we do about it? What battle rages in our schools?

6. Name some occultish practices that God forbids. Why is He so adamant about this subject?

7. Think seriously about which obstacles and pitfalls trip you up most often. What can you do?

Open Sharing: Feel free to discuss questions or anything related to the chapter that ministered to members of the group. Let the Holy Spirit lead you.

Fire-Starter's Preparation

Spend time alone and together worshiping the Lord. Before and after, record your thoughts and feelings in a journal. Write down changes you notice in your life.

Notes

Chapter Twelve

FOREVER TRANSFORMED

Christian worship is the most momentous, the most urgent, the
most glorious action that can take place in human life.

KARL BARTH[1]

WORSHIP!

Most Momentous—significant, decisive, pivotal.

Most Urgent—compelling, imperative, crucial.

Most Glorious—superb, transcendent, sublime.

And the superlative of all these adjectives describes worship.
Does it hold such an esteemed position in your life? For a Christian, worship should form the hub around which the wheel of life
revolves. His or her time ceases to be controlled by the routine of
living. A worshiper has renounced the habit of just going through
the motions in the first few moments of a Sunday morning church

169

service. It's easy to do outward spiritual calisthenics without the heart even getting warmed up.

As you well know, total transformation does not happen overnight, or without struggle. But no one who has entered the presence of Almighty God has ever left untouched by His hand.

> In holy intimacy, the true worshipper comes face to face with God and he is transformed by the glory. If the corporate worship in the church leaves people unchanged, the church is not really worshipping. If what goes on in a church service does not spur the saints to greater obedience, call it what you will, it isn't worship. Worship always results in a transformation and the church is edified by it.[2]

Moses' experience at the burning bush forever changed him and left him with a new purpose in life. The prophet Isaiah, another man who looked up to see the glory of God, was changed. He became the most well known Old Testament prophet because of the revelation God gave him of the coming Messiah. Ezekiel saw God's glory and became the prophet and watchman of Israel. Each transformation occurred after a vision of the glory of the Lord. The same holds true for us today.

After we finally acknowledge that God alone can satisfy the hunger within and we set our hearts to become worshipers, the process of change begins. He smoothes some of the rough edges that prevent us from enjoying Him. Then one day while our spirits are gazing up, we, too, catch a glimpse of the glory of the Lord. Seeing the "utter and awesome holiness of God" and "ourselves against the backdrop of that holiness," our lives cannot help but be forever changed.[3]

You may remember from the triangles in Part One that worship is the motivational aspect of a relationship with God. It keeps the fires of the heart burning brightly, regardless of situations in which we find ourselves. Worship lifts the spirit to soar heavenward. Although our lives may be filled with physical suffering, we can still rejoice. Passionate, fiery worship, when balanced with a well-founded knowledge and steadfast covenant with the Lord, makes the following promise a reality: "But in all these things we overwhelmingly conquer through Him who loved us" (Romans 8:37).

The apostle Paul provides a prime example of such an overcomer who underwent a radical change. With the misguided zeal of a legalistic Pharisee, Saul (his Hebrew name) sought authorization from the highest Jewish officials to persecute believers. One day, he had an experience on the road to Damascus that blinded him for three days (Acts 9:3–9). It changed him spiritually forever. He met the resurrected Christ! Three days of darkness marked the beginning of a lifetime of enlightened worship for Paul. From then on, even amidst the harshest circumstances possible, he maintained profound inner joy and wrote a large portion of the New Testament. Paul could write with confidence because he had learned the truth for himself.

> In far more labors, in far more imprisonments, beaten times without number, often in danger of death. Five times I received from the Jews thirty-nine lashes. Three times I was beaten with rods, once I was stoned, three times I was shipwrecked, a night and a day I have spent in the deep. I have been on frequent journeys, in dangers from rivers, dangers from robbers, dangers from my countrymen, dangers from the Gentiles, dangers in the city, dangers in the wilderness, dangers on the sea, dangers among false brethren; I have been in labor and hardship, through many sleepless nights, in hunger and thirst, often without food, in cold and exposure.
>
> —2 Corinthians 11:23–27

Amazing, isn't it, that throughout all his tribulations, Paul continued to say, "Rejoice evermore" (1 Thessalonians 5:16, kjv)? Whether his walk with the Lord led him over mountains or through valleys, Paul's ability to worship remained steadfast. He produced rich, abundant fruit wherever he went.

As our personal lives of worship progress from glory to glory, as we discover what it really means to abide in God's presence, the Holy Spirit will bring forth the fruit of the Spirit in us, too. We mentioned them earlier: love, joy, peace, longsuffering, gentleness, goodness, faith, meekness, temperance (Galatians 5:22–23, KJV).

Note the condition Jesus placed on our ability to bear fruit:

> I am the vine, you are the branches; he who abides in Me and I in him, he bears much fruit, for apart from Me you can do nothing.…If you abide in Me, and My words abide in you, ask whatever you wish, and it will be done for you. My Father is glorified by this, that you bear much fruit, and so prove to be My disciples.
>
> —JOHN 15:5, 7–8

The transformation in us also resembles the process by which a plain stone, in the hands of a master sculptor, becomes a work of art. Michelangelo once described his talent as an ability to see the masterpiece hidden within the block of marble and then to release it. God sees a saint contained within our rough exteriors. As we abide in Jesus and worship Him, the Holy Spirit brings forth another masterpiece for His glory.

Coupled with this freedom to worship comes a greater responsibility and renewed call to holiness. Only after God commanded Moses to build a tabernacle, the pattern for all true worship, did He say, "You shall be holy, for I the LORD your God am holy" (Leviticus 19:2). The Lord knew that neither the Israelites nor we could even begin to fulfill this command until we learned to worship.

As God leads us toward holiness, we will fail, but He can still use periods of reversal to develop character. If we view them from the proper perspective, if we endure with patience, if we continue to rise above failures and rejoice in our total dependency upon Him, then our lives will become a pleasing fragrance to Him. We needn't grow frustrated or discouraged because of newly discovered shortcomings. Rather, we can take heart in God's faithfulness and draw near to Him. In His presence is "fullness of joy" and in His right hand there are "pleasures forever" (Psalm 16:11).

Erwin Lutzer, author of *Failure—The Back Door to Success*, emphasizes the advantages of occasional setbacks:

The fuel of worship is a true vision of the greatness of God; the fire that makes the fuel burn white-hot is the quickening of the Holy Spirit; the furnace made alive and warm by the flame of truth is our renewed spirit; the resulting heat of our affections is powerful worship, pushing its way out in confessions, longings, acclamations, tears, songs, shouts, bowed heads, lifted hands and obedient lives.[4]

Yes, worship accomplishes great things for God, both in and through the believer, but we fight a tremendous battle to do it. Why? Why has Satan gone to such great lengths to distort the truth of this glorious encounter and distract us from it? Why has he tried to make believers apprehensive about coming into the presence of Almighty God? Simple. He knows the power of worship. Do you remember? Before Lucifer fell from heaven, he had a very important job as the anointed cherub. He led worship of the Father.

When the body of Christ begins to worship God as He intends, we will experience the greatest move of the Holy Spirit this world has ever imagined. Satan will do everything he can to prevent such a spiritual explosion, but his plans are doomed. The Word promises that when the Bridegroom returns to receive His bride, the church, she will be spotless! Through perfect love—worship, based on knowledge, leading to covenant—God will accomplish this feat in us.

Let's do an honest self-evaluation. How appreciative are we of God's "unspeakable gift"? Do we, like the canines Monarch and Mitzi, respond to our Master? Do we do so with open gratitude? Exuberant anticipation? Eagerness to please Him? Can others see from looking at our day-to-day lives that an all-consuming love for God motivates us? Do we burn like lights in a darkened world? Worshipers not only burn, they glow.

Worship involves giving something back to God. In a spirit of thankfulness, we present Him a gift for who He is and what He has done because "the Lord has done great things for us; We are glad" (Psalm 126:3). Some people wonder what they can give the Lord that He doesn't already have. He owns the Earth in all its fullness. What more is left? The best thing we can give Him is what He gave us: our lives, our free will. Out of love, we can submit them to Him.

Just as the Hebrew priests offered sacrifices in the tabernacle and Jesus offered Himself as the ultimate sacrifice on the cross, we relinquish any rights we think we have to ourselves. What does the God of the whole universe want with us? He wants us to be washed in the blood of the Lamb, filled with His Spirit, and consecrated to serve Him.

Paul wrote in Romans that this kind of sacrifice leads not to physical death, as it did for Jesus, but to a brand new life—one of service.

> Therefore I urge you, brethren, by the mercies of God, to present your bodies a living and holy sacrifice, acceptable to God, which is your spiritual service of worship.
> —ROMANS 12:1

Although He does want us to soar in worship's abandon, we must still come down to Earth. In other words, we must not wind up so heavenly minded that we're of no earthly good, as Oliver Wendell Holmes quipped. Mountaintops of praise and worship enable us to return to the valleys and be loving servants!

Ronald Allen and Gordon Borror noted the close tie between worship and service:

> How are we fully to love one another as Christ loved us if we do not practice loving God? How can we possibly love lost mankind except to see them as God sees them? We cannot see from His point of view until we know Him.[5]

As we allow the Lord to develop within us the heart attitudes of a true servant, we become more like Jesus. He said:

> Whoever wishes to become great among you shall be your servant; and whoever wishes to be first among you shall be slave of all. For even the Son of Man did not come to be served, but to serve, and to give His life a ransom for many.
> —MARK 10:43–45

Effective Christian service flows from a heart that acknowledges the glory, majesty, and power of One who is King, yet who came to serve. As we understand this and learn to love Him deeply, we won't have to drum up motivation. Dead obedience will fall by the wayside. Rather, our spirits will radiate the joy of salvation in all our work. The King of servanthood will empower us to worship in everything we do, which in turn, leads to a greater desire to continue serving. Then, "the joy of the LORD is your strength" (Nehemiah 8:10).

When we ripen into such spiritual maturity, we experience new freedom. In a sense, something cushions us from the anxieties of the world. No longer do fear and frustration keep us chained to distorted views of Christian service. Cold, ritualistic religion with its infamous good deed-doing melts under a heart aflame. Fiery worship gives birth to genuine service that springs out of a purified heart.

Service never replaces worship; rather, service results from worship. Therein lies the key to reaching out to others with an attitude of gratitude. Worship first; serve second. The divine order is important. We see this same association in the words of Jesus during His temptation in the wilderness: "Go, Satan! For it is written, 'You shall worship the LORD your God, and serve Him only'" (Matthew 4:10).

As we have seen, worship is a spontaneous and dynamic expression of heartfelt emotion—a response on our part to God's greatness. As A. P. Gibbs said, "Worship is the occupation of the heart, not with its needs or even with its blessings, but with God, Himself."[6] That means referring to ourselves with modesty, as King David did after he learned what great things were in store for him.

> For thou, Lord GOD, knowest thy servant. For thy word's sake, and according to thine own heart, hast thou done all these great things, to make thy servant know them. Wherefore thou art great, O LORD God: for there is none like thee, neither is there any God beside thee.
>
> —2 SAMUEL 7:20–22, KJV

Can we rest in God's presence long enough to let Him create pure hearts in us? Any other form of service turns out to be a cheap imitation. It fades away. By comparison, "The work done by a worshiper will have eternity in it."[7]

A word of caution: we can get pretty adept at counterfeit ministry. In order to further our own selfish ambitions, we can even fool ourselves. Our efforts to serve God lead us to put up a façade, a kind of whitewashed fence for others to see. We slip on an attractive covering to camouflage our old, hateful selves. No inner change of heart occurs daily. We lack sincerity, one could say.

A brief study of the word *sincere* will give us a better understanding of counterfeit service. Sincerity is related to a phrase *"sine cero,"* meaning "without wax."[8] In ancient Greece, when a master sculptor completed a flawless piece of art, he had no need to cover it with wax to give a smooth appearance. Less skilled sculptors melted wax to hide the cracks and chips in the "untrue" marble. The most reputable craftsmen marked their expensive creations *"sine cero."* Could God hang a *"sine cero"* tag on us?

We gain sincerity through communion with Him. In His holy presence, He exposes the false and sanctifies us through repentance. He alone can keep us from becoming polished apples with rotten cores! Genuine fruit of the Spirit—love, joy, peace, long-suffering, gentleness, meekness, and temperance—grow only in the rich environment of the cross.

God the Father has given every believer all he or she will ever need to serve Him, that is, when we come to Him in our weakness. We don't have to work for Him in our own strength. We needn't depend on our own abilities. How, then, can we accomplish what He gives us to do? In the book of Zechariah, we find God's answer, which is just as true for us today: "This is the word of the LORD to Zerubbabel saying, 'Not by might nor by power, but by My Spirit,' says the LORD of hosts" (Zechariah 4:6).

Ministry, then, is accomplished through the anointing of the Holy Spirit. As our worship experience with the Spirit develops, our capacity for service expands. We become extensions of His love. His gifts pass through our hands to the surrounding world, effecting changes in it.

"Truly, those who worship most will serve God best, and only the Spirit can supply the power for both."[9]

God the Father wants His children to continue the task of bringing the gospel to the world! He then builds up His church through the anointing and gifts of the Holy Spirit. The church has one Head—Jesus.

> He also is head of the body, the church; and He is the beginning, the firstborn from the dead; so that He Himself will come to have first place in everything.
>
> —COLOSSIANS 1:18

For the shepherding and perfecting of His body, Jesus established certain governmental offices, commonly referred to as "the five-fold ministry." Paul enumerated them in his letter to the Ephesian church: the apostle, prophet, evangelist, pastor, and teacher. Not everyone is called to be the pastor of a church or an international evangelist like Billy Graham. Yet, God summons each of us to serve and has given us at least one supernatural gift to compensate for our weakness.

> Now there are varieties of gifts, but the same Spirit. And there are varieties of ministries, and the same Lord. There are varieties of effects, but the same God who works all things in all persons. But to each one is given the manifestation of the Spirit for the common good...one and the same Spirit works all these things, distributing to each one individually just as He wills.
>
> —1 CORINTHIANS 12:4–7, 11

> For just as we have many members in one body and all the members do not have the same function, so we, who are many, are one body in Christ, and individually members one of another. Since we have gifts that differ according to the grace given to us, each of us is to exercise them accordingly.
>
> —ROMANS 12:4–6

A certain unity binds Christians together, but we don't become carbon copies of one another. The Spirit enhances our individual roles. He helps every person become a productive "cell" of a healthy spiritual body that carries out the work of Christ in the world.

When others view the living, vibrant church, the power of Jesus should be evident for all to see. We can't claim any credit. Instead, His Spirit simply moves through us as we yield to Him. Christian service of this sort reflects a wonderful partnership in which we work *with* God and not *for* Him. We trust not in human strength alone, "for we are the true circumcision, who worship in the Spirit of God and glory in Christ Jesus and put no confidence in the flesh" (Philippians 3:3).

The phrase in Zechariah 4:6, "by My Spirit, says the LORD of hosts," reminds us that a lifestyle of worship fills up the wellspring from which loving, dynamic Christian service flows. No more feelings of being driven to drudgery so we can fall asleep with clear consciences. Rather, service bubbles out of our innermost beings in gratitude to our precious Lord. So let's rejoice in our union with Jesus. He is the Fountainhead of this mighty roaring river of life. We can be confident in His ability to fulfill all He has promised to do through us. Oh, what a relief!

How about if we take one last look into the heavenlies, that the fire blazing in our hearts may intensify? But first, think back to the chapter entitled "Visions of Glory," where we saw the Father seated on His heavenly throne. We also caught a glimpse of Jesus as both the sacrificial Lamb and the soon-coming King. We witnessed, with the apostle John, the countless thousands worshiping Father and Son in the most magnificent service ever to be assembled. The Holy Spirit wants to unveil yet one more scene in our heavenward gaze—the spectacle that will take place at the beginning of God's judgment.

When the Lamb broke the seventh seal, there was silence in heaven for about half an hour.
—REVELATION 8:1

A holy hush will settle over heaven! Think of that! For the first time since God spoke the universe into being, angelic accolades will cease. No more cries of, "Holy, holy, holy!" ringing forth from the throne room (Revelation 4:8). No more heavenly hurrahs accompanying the saints' praises. An absence of sound will permeate the universe.

Have you ever wondered what significance this moment holds in God's plan? Thousands of years ago, He commanded in Psalm 46:10, "Be still, and know that I am God" (KJV). With this passage of Revelation dawns the fulfillment of this psalm. Every being in heaven, in Earth, and under the Earth—even Satan—will be silent when God the Father rises from His throne to pronounce judgment. For one half hour, every eye will be riveted on Him as He stands in all His unimaginable glory.

A clue to this ultimate event appears in another psalm: "Thou didst cause judgment to be heard from heaven; the earth feared, and was still, when God arose to judgment, to save all the meek of the earth" (Psalm 76:8–9, KJV).

Later, the Lord revealed to the prophet Daniel the wonders that will follow.

> I kept looking, and that horn was waging war with the saints and overpowering them until the Ancient of Days came and judgment was passed in favor of the saints of the Highest One, and the time arrived when the saints took possession of the kingdom.
>
> —DANIEL 7:21–22

After God the Father stands, He will assume His rightful place on the throne of judgment.

> I kept looking Until thrones were set up, And the Ancient of Days took His seat; His vesture was like white snow And the hair of His head like pure wool. His throne was ablaze with flames, Its wheels were a burning fire. A river of fire was flowing And coming out from before Him; Thousands upon thousands were attending Him, And myriads upon myriads were standing before Him. The court sat, And the books were opened.
>
> —DANIEL 7:9–10

Silence.

Awesome…Deafening…Quiet.

So great is our glorious God of heaven that countless numbers will be speechless before Him. The Holy Spirit is working to prepare us for that day when time draws to a close. He longs to teach us to worship in reverential wonder and yet to worship in exuberant gratitude—with the spontaneous joy of Monarch in our opening story.

We have the opportunity of the ages. God gives us freedom to choose. How wise He is! We can run eagerly into His loving embrace or turn our backs on Him. Which will it be?

FIRE-SEEKER'S COMPANION

Questions for Group Interaction or Individual Reflection

1. Karl Barth said, "Worship is the most _____, the most _____, the most _____ action that can take place in human life." Define further each of these terms. Do they describe your attitude toward worship?

2. What happens to someone who learns to worship? Name some saints who experienced this. What is the fruit of the Spirit, and how is it produced? What will cause a failure to produce fruit?

3. Why do you face such a struggle to worship? What will happen if the body of Christ worships anyway? Can others see a positive difference in you? What difference should they see?

4. What can the saint give God who owns everything? Mountaintops of praise and worship enable you to get down in the valleys—and do what? Why? "Service never _____ worship. Service _____from worship."

5. Genuine service happens by what power? Who can serve God best? Do we all serve in the same way? Why or why not?

6. When will total silence fall over heaven? For how long? How will the Earth respond? By contrast, what will happen to the humble?

7. Describe the scene when the Ancient of Days takes His seat. What does He look like, and who is there with Him? How is God preparing you for that moment? Are you ready? Write a love letter to Him and pour out your heart.

Open Sharing: Feel free to discuss questions or anything related to the chapter that ministered to members of the group. Let the Holy Spirit lead you.

Fire-Starter's Preparation

Spend time alone and together worshiping the Lord. Before and after, record your thoughts and feelings in a journal. Write down changes you notice in your life.

Notes

BIBLIOGRAPHY

Holy Bible, New American Standard Version. Nashville, TN: The Lockman Foundation and Thomas Nelson Publishers, 1977.

Allen, Ronald and Borror, Gordon. *Worship, Rediscovering the Missing Jewel.* Portland, OR: Multnomah Press, 1982.

Cornwall, Judson. *Elements of Worship.* Plainfield, NJ: Bridge Publishing, Inc., 1985.

Cornwall, Judson. *Let Us Worship.* Plainfield, NJ: Bridge Publishing, Inc., 1983.

Gibbs, Alfred P. *Worship, The Christian's Highest Occupation.* Dubuque, IA: Walterick Publishers Inc., n.d.

Jennings, Theodore W. *Life as Worship.* Grand Rapids, MI: Wm. B. Eerdmans Publishing Co., 1982.

MacArthur, John F., Jr. *The Ultimate Priority.* Chicago, IL: Moody Press, 1983.

Mears, Henrietta C. *What the Bible Is All About.* Ventura, CA: Regal, 1983.

Mumford, Bob. *Entering and Enjoying Worship.* Manna Christian Outreach, 1975.

Nee, Watchman. *The Spiritual Man.* Richmond, VA: Christian Fellowship Publishers, Inc., 1968.

Pink, Arthur W. *Profiting from the Word.* Carlisle, PA: The Banner of Truth Trust, 1985.

Piper, John. *Desiring God.* Portland, OR: Multnomah Press, 1986.

Taylor, Jack R. *The Hallelujah Factor.* Nashville, TN: Broadman Press, 1983.

Tozer, A. W. *Worship: The Missing Jewel of the Evangelical Church.* Philadelphia, PA: Christian Publications, Inc., n.d.

Wiersbe, Warren W. *Real Worship.* Nashville, TN: Oliver-Nelson Books, 1986.

NOTES

Chapter 1
Prelude to Worship

1. Based on Alfred P. Gibbs, *Worship: The Christian's Highest Occupation* (Kansas City, KS: Walterick Publications, n.d.), 63–64.

2. A. W. Tozer, *Worship: The Missing Jewel of the Evangelical Church* (Harrisburg, PA: Christian Publications, n.d.), 11.

3. Blaise Pascal, *Pascal's Pensées*, trans. by W. F. Trotter (E. P. Dutton, 1958), 113.

4. Judson Cornwall, *Let Us Worship* (South Plainfield, NJ: Bridge Publishing, Inc., 1985), 11.

5. Malcolm Smith, *Rise Above Burnout* (San Antonio, TX; Malcolm Smith Ministries Teaching Cassettes, n.d.), tape 1.

6. Judson Cornwall, *The Elements of Worship* (South Plainfield, NJ: Bridge Publishing, Inc., 1983), 11–12.

7. Tozer.

8. Definition available online at http://strongsnumbers.com/hebrew/7812.htm (accessed 1/14/09).

9. Definition available online at http://www.biblestudytools.net/Lexicons/Greek/grk.cgi?number=4352 (accessed 1/14/09).

10. Cornwall, *Let Us Worship*, 51.

11. Merriam-Webster's Collegiate Dictionary, eleventh edition (Springfield, MA: Merriam-Webster, Inc., 2003), s.v. "worship."

12. Tozer, 7–9.

13. William Temple, *The Hope of a New World*, 30; cited by John F. MacArthur, *The Ultimate Priority* (Chicago: Moody Press, 1983), 87.

14. John F. MacArthur, Jr., *The Ultimate Priority* (Chicago: Mood Press, 1983), 87.

15. Tozer, 9.

16. Cornwall, *Let Us Worship*, 45.

Chapter 2
A Delicate Balance

1. Sarah Doherty quote available at *Dave's Unfamiliar Quotations*, http://www.mrbecker.com/quotations.html#contents (accessed December 17, 2008).

2. John Piper, *Desiring God* (Multnomah Press, 1986), 65.

Chapter 3
Making Ready the Heart

1. Chuck Swindoll, "Growing Deep in the Christian Life" Message Series (Insight for Living, Fullerton, California, 1987).

2. Gibbs, 51.

Chapter 5
Getting to Know Him

1. Cornwall, Elements of Worship, 199.

2. Definition of *El Shaddai* available online at http://www.hebrew-4christians.com/Names_of_G-d/El/el.html (accessed 1/15/09).

3. Bob Mumford, *Entering and Enjoying Worship* (Ft. Lauderdale, FL: Manna Christian Outreach, 1975), preface.

4. Gibbs, 157–176, 189–199.

5. Piper, 67.

Chapter 6
Of Tabernacles and Temples

1. MacArthur, Jr., *The Ultimate Priority* (Chicago, IL: Moody Press, 1983), 79.

2. Cornwall, *Let Us Worship*, 172.

3. Henrietta C. Mears, *What the Bible Is All About* (Ventura, CA: Regal, 1983).

4. Definition of *daka* available online at http://www.studylight.org/lex/heb/view.cgi?number=01792 (accessed 1/16/09).

Chapter 7

Prayer: The Heartbeat of Worship

1. Cornwall, *Elements of Worship*, 99.

2. Theodore W. Jennings, *Life as Worship* (Grand Rapids, MI: Wm. B. Eerdmans Publishing Co., 1982), 65.

3. Cornwall, *Elements of Worship*, 82.

4. Leonard Ravenhill, *Revival Praying* (Minneapolis, MN: Bethany House Publishers, 1962), in *Last Days Magazine* (Last Days Ministries, Fall 1987), 26.

5. Arthur W. Pink, *Profiting from the Word* (Carlisle, PA: The Banner of Truth Trust, 1985), 51.

6. C. H. Spurgeon quote may be found in John MacArthur, Jr., "True Worship: Part 3 of the John MacArthur Study Guide Collection," http://www.biblebb.com/files/MAC/TWCH7.HTM (accessed December 19, 2008).

7. John Wesley quote may be found in Kevin A. Miller and Russ Reid, "When You Need a Break," July 11, 2007, *Building Church Leaders*, http://www.buildingchurchleaders.com/articles/1988/le-1988-002-4.36.html (accessed December 19, 2008).

8. Pink, 52.

9. Ibid, 49.

10. Jennings, 67.

Chapter 8

A Day-by-Day Lifestyle

1. Ronald Allen and Gordon Borror, *Worship: Rediscovering the Missing Jewel* (Eugene, OR: Wipf and Stock Publishers, 2001), 132.

2. Cornwall, *Elements of Worship*, 113.

3. Cornwall, *Let Us Worship*, p. 33.

4. Allen and Borror, 23–24.

Chapter 9

Celebrating God Together

1. Allen and Borror, 19.

2. Ibid, 189.

3.   Jennings, preface.

4.   Cornwall, *Elements of Worship*, 108.

5.   MacArthur, Jr., 121–122.

6.   Warren Wiersbe, *Real Worship* (Nashville, TN: Oliver-Nelson Books, 1986), 180.

7.   Gibbs, 17.

Chapter 10
Obstacles

1.   Mumford, 25.

2.   Gibbs, 216.

3.   Ibid, 233.

4.   Cornwall, *Elements of Worship*, 116.

Chapter 11
Pitfalls

1.   Gibbs, 145.

2.   Tozer, 5–6.

3.   *Insight: The Washington Times*, date unknown.

4.   Cornwall, *Elements of Worship*, 117.

Chapter 12
Forever Transformed

1.   Karl Barth quote may be found at "Worship," *PraiseFM*, http://www.praisefm.org/worship.cfm (accessed December 22, 2008).

2.   MacArthur, Jr., 155.

3.   Ibid, 86.

4.   Piper, 66.

5.   Allen and Borror, 38.

6.   Gibbs, 14.

7.   Tozer, 14.

8.   Definition of *sine cero* available online at www.websters-online-dictionary.org/mu/museum.html (accessed 1/16/09).

9.   Gibbs, 199.

ABOUT THE AUTHOR

James P. Gills, M.D., received his medical degree from Duke University Medical Center in 1959. He served his ophthalmology residency at Wilmer Ophthalmological Institute of Johns Hopkins University from 1962–1965. Dr. Gills founded the St. Luke's Cataract and Laser Institute in Tarpon Springs, Florida, and has performed more cataract and lens implant surgeries than any other eye surgeon in the world. Since establishing his Florida practice in 1968, he has been firmly committed to embracing new technology and perfecting the latest cataract surgery techniques. In 1974, he became the first eye surgeon in the U.S. to dedicate his practice to cataract treatment through the use of intraocular lenses. Dr. Gills has been recognized in Florida and throughout the world for his professional accomplishments and personal commitment to helping others. He has been recognized by the readers of *Cataract & Refractive Surgery Today* as one of the top 50 cataract and refractive opinion leaders.

As a world-renowned ophthalmologist, Dr. Gills has received innumerable medical and educational awards. In 2005, he was especially honored to receive the Duke Medical Alumni Association's Humanitarian Award. In 2007, he was blessed with a particularly treasured double honor. Dr. Gills was elected to the Johns Hopkins Society of Scholars and was also selected to receive the Distinguished Medical Alumnus Award, the highest honor bestowed by Johns Hopkins School of Medicine. Dr. Gills thereby became the first physician in the country to receive high honors twice in two weeks from the prestigious Johns Hopkins University in Baltimore.

In the years 1994 through 2004, Dr. Gills was listed in *The Best Doctors in America*. As a clinical professor of ophthalmology at the University of South Florida, he was named one of the best Ophthalmologists in America in 1996 by ophthalmic academic leaders nationwide. He has served on the Board of Directors of the American College of Eye Surgeons, the Board of Visitors at Duke University Medical Center, and the Advisory Board of Wilmer Ophthalmological

Institute at Johns Hopkins University. Listed in Marquis' *Who's Who in America*, Dr. Gills was Entrepreneur of the Year 1990 for the State of Florida, received the Tampa Bay Business Hall of Fame Award in 1993, and was given the Tampa Bay Ethics Award from the University of Tampa in 1995. In 1996, he was awarded the prestigious Innovators Award by his colleagues in the American Society of Cataract and Refractive Surgeons. In 2000, he was named Philanthropist of the Year by the National Society of Fundraising Executives, was presented with the Florida Enterprise Medal by the Merchants Association of Florida, was named Humanitarian of the Year by the Golda Meir/Kent Jewish Center in Clearwater, and was honored as Free Enterpriser of the Year by the Florida Council on Economic Education. In 2001, The Salvation Army presented Dr. Gills their prestigious "Others Award" in honor of his lifelong commitment to service and caring.

Virginia Polytechnic Institute, Dr. Gills' alma mater, presented their University Distinguished Achievement Award to him in 2003. In that same year, Dr. Gills was appointed by Governor Jeb Bush to the Board of Directors of the Florida Sports Foundation. In 2004, Dr. Gills was invited to join the prestigious Florida Council of 100, an advisory committee reporting directly to the governor on various aspects of Florida's public policy affecting the quality of life and the economic well-being of all Floridians.

While Dr. Gills has many accomplishments and varied interests, his primary focus is to restore physical vision to patients and to bring spiritual enlightenment through his life. Guided by his strong and enduring faith in Jesus Christ, he seeks to encourage and comfort the patients who come to St. Luke's and to share his faith whenever possible. It was through sharing his insights with patients that he initially began writing on Christian topics. An avid student of the Bible for many years, he now has authored nineteen books on Christian living, with over nine million copies in print. With the exception of the Bible, Dr. Gills' books are the most widely requested books in the U.S. prison system. They have been supplied to over two thousand prisons and jails, including every death row facility in the nation. In addition, Dr. Gills has published more than 195 medical articles and

has authored or coauthored ten medical reference textbooks. Six of
those books were bestsellers at the American Academy of Ophthalmology annual meetings.

As an ultra-distance athlete, Dr. Gills participated in forty-six marathons, including eighteen Boston marathons and fourteen 100-mile
mountain runs. In addition, he completed five Ironman Triathlons
in Hawaii and a total of six Double Ironman Triathlons, each within
the thirty-six hour maximum time frame. Dr. Gills has served on the
National Board of Directors of the Fellowship of Christian Athletes
and, in 1991, was the first recipient of their Tom Landry Award. A
passionate athlete, surgeon, and scientist, Dr. Gills is also a member of
the Explorers Club, a prestigious, multi-disciplinary society dedicated
to advancing field research, scientific exploration, and the ideal that it
is vital to preserve the instinct to explore.

Married in 1962, Dr. Gills and his wife, Heather, have raised two
children, Shea and Pit. Shea Gills Grundy, a former attorney and now
full-time mom, is a graduate of Vanderbilt University and Emory Law
School. She and her husband, Shane Grundy, M.D., have four children: twins Maggie and Braddock, Jimmy, and Lily Grace. The Gills'
son, J. Pit Gills, M.D., ophthalmologist, received his medical degree
from Duke University Medical Center and, in 2001, joined the St.
Luke's practice. "Dr. Pit" and his wife, Joy, have three children: Pitzer,
Parker, and Stokes.

THE WRITINGS OF JAMES P. GILLS, M.D.

A BIBLICAL ECONOMICS MANIFESTO (WITH RON H. NASH, PH.D.)
The best understanding of economics aligns with what the Bible teaches on the subject.
ISBN: 978-0-88419-871-0
E-book ISBN: 978-1-59979-925-4

BELIEVE AND REJOICE: CHANGED BY FAITH, FILLED WITH JOY
Observe how faith in God can let us see His heart of joy
ISBN: 978-1-59979-169-2
E-book ISBN: 978-1-61638-727-3

COME UNTO ME: GOD'S CALL TO INTIMACY
Inspired by Dr. Gills' trip to Mt. Sinai, this book explores God's eternal desire for mankind to know Him intimately.
ISBN: 978-1-59185-214-8
E-book ISBN: 978-1-61638-728-0

DARWINISM UNDER THE MICROSCOPE: HOW RECENT SCIENTIFIC
EVIDENCE POINTS TO DIVINE DESIGN
(WITH TOM WOODWARD, PH.D.)
Behold the wonder of it all! The facts glorify our Intelligent Creator!
ISBN: 978-0-88419-925-0
E-book ISBN: 978-1-59979-882-0

THE DYNAMICS OF WORSHIP
Designed to rekindle a passionate love for God, this book gives the *who, what, where, when, why,* and *how* of worship.
ISBN: 978-1-59185-657-3
E-book ISBN: 978-1-61638-725-9

EXCEEDING GRATITUDE FOR THE CREATOR'S PLAN: DISCOVER THE
LIFE-CHANGING DYNAMIC OF APPRECIATION
Standing in awe of the creation and being secure in the knowledge of our heavenly hope, the thankful believer abounds in appreciation for the Creator's wondrous plan.
ISBN: 978-1-59979-155-5
E-book ISBN: 978-1-61638-729-7

GOD'S PRESCRIPTION FOR HEALING: FIVE DIVINE GIFTS OF HEALING
Explore the wonders of healing by design, now and forevermore.
ISBN: 978-1-59185-286-5
E-book ISBN: 978-1-61638-730-3

Imaginations: More Than You Think

Focusing our thoughts will help us grow closer to God.
ISBN: 978-1-59185-609-2
E-book ISBN: 978-1-59979-883-7

Love: Fulfilling the Ultimate Quest

Enjoy a quick refresher course on the meaning and method of God's great gift.
ISBN: 978-1-59979-235-4
E-book ISBN: 978-1-61638-731-7

Overcoming Spiritual Blindness

Jesus + anything = nothing. Jesus + nothing = everything. Here is a book that will help you recognize the many facets of spiritual blindness as you seek to fulfill the Lord's plan for your life.
ISBN: 978-1-59185-607-8
E-book ISBN: 978-1-59979-884-4

Resting In His Redemption

We were created for communion with God. Discover how to rest in His redemption and enjoy a life of divine peace.
ISBN: 978-1-61638-349-7
E-book ISBN: 978-1-61638-425-8

Rx for Worry: A Thankful Heart

Trust your future to the God who is in eternal control.
ISBN: 978-1-59979-090-9
E-book ISBN: 978-1-55979-926-1

The Prayerful Spirit: Passion for God, Compassion for People

Dr. Gills tells how prayer has changed his life as well as the lives of patients and other doctors. It will change your life also!
ISBN: 978-1-59185-215-5
E-book ISBN: 978-1-61638-732-7

The Unseen Essential: A Story for Our Troubled Times...
Part One

This compelling, contemporary novel portrays one man's transformation through the power of God's love.
ISBN: 978-1-59185-810-2
E-book ISBN: 978-1-59979-513-3

Tender Journey: A Story for Our Troubled Times...
Part Two

Be enriched by the popular sequel to *The Unseen Essential*.
ISBN: 978-1-59185-809-6
E-book ISBN: 978-1-59979-509-6

DID YOU ENJOY THIS BOOK?

We at Love Press would be pleased to hear from you if

The Dynamics of Worship

has had an effect on your life or the lives of your loved ones.

Send your letters to:

Love Press

PO Box 1608

Tarpon Springs, FL 34688-1608